The Impact of Oil Pollution on the Environment of the Oil Producing Communities of Nigeria:

A Critical Analysis of the Statutory and Regulatory Provisions in Nigeria

Olubunmi Awoyemi, Ph.D

Independent Law Publishing

ISBN10: 0996011692
ISBN13: 9780996011693

TABLE OF CONTENTS

By Olubunmi Awoyemi, Ph.D* +

INTRODUCTION

This legal treatise discusses the environmental impact of oil pollution on the oil producing communities of Nigeria. A critical analysis of the statutory and regulatory provisions governing oil pollution in Nigeria and a brief comparison of the statutory provisions in Nigeria with those of the United States is undertaken. Throughout this research, the phrase "Niger Delta" is used interchangeably with the phrase "oil producing communities."

This legal treatise examines the history of oil exploration and production in Nigeria and also explores the sources and effects of oil pollution. In addition, a cursory look at the friction among the stakeholders in the oil industry is analyzed and the National Oil Spill Contingency Plan (NOSCP) is discussed. A detailed study of the normative concepts and issues involved are achieved and the issue of corporate self-regulation as enunciated in ISO 14000 is assessed.

---

* Bunmi Awoyemi is a partner in the International Law Firm, M.O. Awoyemi & Co. He attended Ogun State University, Nigeria (LL.B 1997); The Nigerian Law School (B.L 1998); and Tulane Law School (LL.M in Maritime Law 1999, S.J.D./Ph.D 2003). The author is admitted to practice law in New York, is a Solicitor of the Supreme Court of England & Wales, and a Barrister & Solicitor of the Supreme Court of Nigeria. The author has worked for some of the biggest and most prestigious law firms in the United Sates, like Baker & Mckenzie, LLP in the city of Chicago and Holland & Knight, LLP in New York City.

+ David Aweda contributed to some parts of this book. David Aweda is a licensed Professional Realtor and was a Real Estate Manager with Metro Brokers-GMAC Real Estate Inc., Georgia, USA. He attended Obafemi Awolowo University, Nigeria (LL.B. 1997), Tulane Law School (LL.M, 2002) and is a graduate of Metro Brokers/GMAC Real Estate Academy, Georgia.

1.A HISTORICAL BACKGROUND

The Niger Delta covers an area of well over 70,000 square kilometers, which amounts to about 37.75 per cent of Nigeria's total landmass; the coastline extends up to 560 kilometers, roughly two thirds of the entire coastline of Nigeria.[1] It has a population of about 39 million people and more than 40 ethnic groups with links to the linguistic groups of Ijaw, Edo, Igbo, Efik, Ibibio and Oron.[2] It is the largest wetland in Africa, rich in renewable and non-renewable natural resources such as oil, gas, bitumen, timber, wildlife, etc.[3] There are seven littoral states in Nigeria that make up the Niger Delta Region: Akwa-Ibom, Bayelsa, Cross Rivers, Edo, Delta, Rivers and Ondo. Other states that are oil producing, but not in the Niger Delta Region are Abia and Imo States.

Oil was first discovered in Nigeria in 1956 at Oloibiri, a town in what is now called Bayelsa state, in the Niger Delta region.[4] The discovery was made by the Royal /Dutch Shell Group. They were welcomed to the region by the Nigerian government, recognizing the substantial economic benefits Nigeria stood to gain.[5]

Majority of Nigerian petroleum is extracted from the tropical Niger Delta region, of which the Ogoni land is one of the richest oil producing areas in that region in terms of the volume of oil extracted daily.[6] Shell operates a joint venture on behalf of the state-owned Nigerian National Petroleum Corporation (NNPC) with the latter holding fifty-five percent.[7] Nigeria produces an estimated two

---

[1] M.O. Agwu, Community Participation and Sustainable Development in the Niger Delta, British Journal of Education, Society & Behavioural Science, 3(1): 33-46, at 34, (2013)

[2] Id. at 34.

[3] Id.

[4] See. Amnesty International: Nigeria: Claiming rights and resources Injustice, oil and violence in Nigeria http://www.amnesty.org/en/library/asset/AFR44/020/2005/en/dae6fbde-d4b6-11dd-8a23-d58a49c0d652/afr440202005en.html (last accessed August 27, 2014).

[5] See Joshua P. Eaton, The Nigerian Tragedy, Environmental Regulation of Transnational Corporations, And the Human Rights to a Human Environment, 15 B.D. Int'l L.J. 261, 265 (1997).

[6] Id at 265

[7] Id.

million barrels of oil per day, and this production level makes Nigeria OPEC's sixth largest oil exporting country.[8] Oil comprises over ninety percent of Nigeria's export revenues, accounts for around 80% of government revenues, and over 90% of foreign exchange earnings, and provides the Nigerian government with around ten billion dollars per year.[9] Nigeria contains estimated proven oil resources of 22.5 billion barrels.[10] The Niger Delta is said to be one of the world's largest wetlands.[11] These 36,000 square kilometers (14,000 square miles) of marshland, creeks, tributaries and lagoons drain the Niger River into the Atlantic Ocean at the bight of Biafra.[12] It has a very fragile mangrove forest, and the biological diversity of the area is very high.[13] The Niger Delta is "an easily disequilibrated environment, and it has a very sensitive ecosystem."[14]

---

[8] See. Charles Marecic, How Many Wrongs Does It Take To Make A Human Right, 22 Vt. L. Rev. 201, 204 (1997).

[9] See id at 204.

[10] S. P. Stultz-Karim, West Africa Oil and Gas,http://www.times-publications.com/publications/corporate_africa/articles/oil_gas5.html (last accessed August 25th 2014)

[11] Okechukwu Ibeanu, Oiling the Friction: Environmental Conflict Management in the Niger Delta, Nigeria, Environmental Change and Security Project Report, Issue 6, at 20 (Summer 2000) http://www.wilsoncenter.org/topics/pubs/Report6-2.pdf (last accessed August 21st 2014).

[12] Id. at 20.

[13] Id.

[14] Id.

CHAPTER ONE

I. A. Sources of oil pollution in the Niger Delta region

Petroleum provides Nigeria with over eighty percent of government revenues annually thus making oil production central to the survival of the functioning of government.[15] The 1999 constitution of Nigeria provides for basic entitlement to a clean environment. Section 20 of the constitution states: "The state shall protect and improve the environment and safeguard the water, air and land, forest and wildlife of Nigeria." This section unfortunately falls under Chapter II which is a non-binding statement of objectives.

Upstream and downstream petroleum activities span the length and breadth of Nigeria.[16] The upstream or crude oil production part of those activities are concentrated in the following nine Nigerian states: namely, Rivers, Bayelsa, Delta, Edo, Imo, Abia, Akwa-Ibom, Cross-River, and Ondo. These nine states are referred to as the oil producing states or communities.

Petroleum activities include seismic, exploration, production, storage, and transportation by ocean-going vessels and pipelines, as well as refining or processing.[17] The activities vary in intensity in different areas but they are concentrated mainly in the Niger Delta, which is considered environmentally very sensitive to an oil spill in view of the complexity of its ecological setting and endowment.[18] All of the crude petroleum is transported via pipelines to storage depots – terminals within the Niger Delta and areas contiguous to it.[19]

---

[15] Id. at 21.

[16] See. The National Oil Spill Contingency Plan (NOSCP) for Nigeria, by The Sub-committee On Oil Spill Response of the National Action Coordinating Committee of the Forum for Cleaning-Up of The Niger Delta, p 23, 3.0.1, Revised Edition May 2009, http://www.giwacaf.org/userfiles/contingency/18/Nigeria_NOSCP_2009_EN.pdf (last accessed September 6, 2014).

[17] Id. at 23.

[18] Id.

[19] Id.

There are seven terminals out of which five are located along the coastline. These include the Bonny, Forcados, Qua Iboe, Escravos, and Brass terminals.[20] The other two are Oloibiri and Antan terminals, both of which are located off the shoreline – on the Atlantic Ocean.[21] Each of these seven terminals has one or more loading points – Single Buoy Mooring (SBMs) where large capacity oceangoing vessels moor to load.[22]

The sources of oil pollution in Nigeria are primarily from the oil fields. Water resources in the Nigeria Delta region are polluted from well blow-outs, indiscriminate direct discharge of production waters, refinery effluents on land and water, leaks from pipelines and storage tanks, spills during storage and loading operations at terminals, and discharge of waste oil into waters from motorized boats.[23] Groundwater is also contaminated by liquids from surface impoundment or spills from storage tanks, pipelines, improperly closed oil wells and poorly constructed injection wells.[24] High-pressure pipelines crisscross villages carrying crude oil and most of the pipelines are laid above the ground surface.[25] In 1998, a pipeline leak that flooded the village of Jesse exploded killing over 1000 people.[26]

The National Oil Spill Contingency Plan (NOSCP) document confirms the state of affairs described above. It noted that the actual storage at any time in these terminals averages above 65% of its total capacity.[27] On the average, between 65 to 100 or more vessels of

---

[20] Id.

[21] Id.

[22] Id.

[23] See. Ambrose O. O. Ekpu, Environmental Impact of Oil on Water: A Comparative Overview of the Law and Policy in the United States and Nigeria, 24 Denv. J. Int'l L. & Pol'y 55, 59 (1995).

[24] Id. at 59.

[25] See Okechukwu Ibeanu, Environmental Change and Security Project Report, Issue 6, at 23 (Summer 2000)

[26] Id. at 23.

[27] See. The National Oil Spill Contingency Plan (NOSCP) for Nigeria, by The Sub-committee On Oil Spill Response of the National Action Coordinating Committee of the Forum for Cleaning-Up of The Niger Delta, at 24, 3.0.3, Revised Edition May 2009,

average capacity of 750,000.00 barrels visit the shores of Nigeria to load crude petroleum in one month.[28] The pipelines through which crude oil is transported from various gathering points to the respective terminals and from the individual terminals to the SBMs sum up to several hundreds of kilometers in length, and crisscross the maze of creeks and coastal areas of the Niger Delta.[29]

The NOSCP document acknowledges that there are about 1,665 producing wells and 616 wells capable of producing in Nigeria.[30] Most of these wells are concentrated within the Niger Delta and the contiguous area (including the coastal areas).[31] Of the producing wells, 1045 are located within the land/swamp area of the Delta while 620 are offshore.[32] The NOSCP document also confirms that the risks associated with the facilities described above would primarily be oil spillage due to the following reasons:

a. Tank failure in any of the terminals.

b. Rupture of major delivery pipelines.

c. Tanker accident within the Nigerian waters.

d. Oil well blowout.

e. Marketing of refined products

f. Human error, and

g. Sabotage.[33]

Another major source of pollution in the region is gas flaring. Nigeria flares more than 76% of its total gas output which is the

---

http://www.giwacaf.org/userfiles/contingency/18/Nigeria_NOSCP_2009_EN.pdf (last accessed September 6, 2014).

[28] Id at 24.

[29] Id.

[30] Id. at 24, 3.0.4.

[31] Id.

[32] Id.

[33] Id at 24, 3.0.4.

highest anywhere in the world, and is said to account for 28% of total gas flared worldwide.[34]

1. B. Effects of oil pollution on Niger Delta Region

The impact of oil production activities includes damage to aquatic life, aesthetic values, recreation, swimming, navigation and human health.[35] Farmlands are also destroyed.

The effect of oil pollution on the Niger Delta region was heralded by the plight of the Ogoni people of Rivers state. The Ogoni like most of rural Nigeria, lack access to potable water, and their major sources of water for drinking are rivers, streams and groundwater.[36] They live a subsistence lifestyle relying on the river for drinking water, food source (seafood), domestic use and farming on the formerly fertile delta land.[37]The land has value to the Niger Delta people beyond the possessory right.[38] It is claimed that the multinational oil company, Shell's business practices in this region rendered the Ogoni soil not farmable, the Ogoni water undrinkable and oil spills from antiquated equipment have polluted their waters.[39] Badly constructed canals and causeways built to facilitate activities of oil companies have devastated the hydrology of the region causing flooding, and also letting saline waters of the Atlantic into freshwater sources

---

[34] See. Emeka Duruigbo, Managing Oil Revenues for Socio-Economic Development in Nigeria: The Case for Community-Based Trust Funds, N.C. J. INT'L L. & COM. REG, Vol. 30, footnote 48, pp 123, 130, https://www.law.unc.edu/components/handlers/document.ashx?category=24&subcategory=52&cid=730 (last accessed on August 18, 2014) (citing, <http://www.ecotopics.com/articles/nigerian_oil.htm> (last modified Sep. 20, 2004) Abiodun Raufu, Nigerian Oil Workers & Families Rage Against Foreign Companies: Citizen Leaders Say Compensation Must Cover Health Damage from Four Decades of Gas Flaring, ECOTOPICS INTERNATIONAL NEWS SERVICE).

[35] See. Ambrose O.O. Ekpu, Environmental Impact of Oil on Water: A Comparative Overview of the Law and Policy in the United States and Nigeria, 24 Denv. J. Int'l L. & Pol'y at 62.

[36] Id. at 63.

[37] See Charles Marecic, How Many Wrongs Does It Take To Make A Human Right, 22 Vt. L. Rev. at 206.

[38] Id at 206.

[39] Id.

thereby increasing the scarcity of drinking water and killing many species of plants, animal and fish.[40]

The New York Times in a stinging editorial on August 14th, 2014, delivered a damning and scathing criticism of the failure of the Nigerian government to implement the United Nations Environment Program (UNEP) Report's recommendations on the restoration of the environment of the Ogoni people of the Niger Delta 3 years after the report was made public.[41] The New York Times observed that despite the fact that the UNEP's report of 2011 issued a comprehensive assessment of shocking levels of pollution in the oil-producing region of Ogoni land in Nigeria, little appears to have been done.[42] According to the editorial, the 2011 UNEP report said that it would take 30 years to repair the damage.[43] The editorial took note of the fact that the week before the editorial, Amnesty International joined other groups in issuing a damning follow-up by accusing the Nigerian government and the Shell Oil Company of essentially ignoring the entire problem.[44]

The New York Times editorial pointed to the part of the United Nations study which found cancer-causing benzene present in drinking water at 900 times the World Health Organization guidelines.[45] The editorial went down memory lane to discuss the 1995 sham trial and execution of celebrated environmental activist and poet Ken Saro-Wiwa and eight others who had protested oil exploitation in Ogoniland.[46] The editorial stated that those executions remain one of the darkest blots on Nigeria's history.[47]

---

[40] See Okechukwu Ibeanu. Environmental Change and Security Project Report. Issue 6. at 23.

[41] Oil's Devastating Legacy in Nigeria, By The Editorial Board, New York Times, (Aug. 14, 2014) http://www.nytimes.com/2014/08/15/opinion/oils-devastating-legacy-in-nigeria.html?emc=edit_ty_20140814&nl=opinion&nlid=55298393&_r=3 (last accessed on September 17, 2014)

[42] Id.

[43] Id.

[44] Id.

[45] Id.

[46] Id.

[47] Id.

The New York Times editorial observed that it was reconciliation talks with the Ogoni people that sparked the idea of an environmental assessment of the region, which led to the 2011 report, which Shell paid for.[48] The editorial noted that Amnesty International had accused Shell of shirking responsibility for the cleanup mandated by the United Nations report.[49]The editorial stated that one of the costs of Shell's past oil exploitation activities is the Ogoni people's stolen health and poisoned environment.[50]

The New York Times editorial acknowledged that in response to the 2011 UNEP report, the Nigerian government did establish a Hydrocarbon Pollution Restoration Project, which Amnesty International says has not amounted to much.[51]

The New York Times pointed to the sufferings of the Ogonis for generations,[52] and posited that it is unacceptable for the Nigerian government and the oil industry to drag their feet under those circumstances.[53] The New York Times called upon the Nigerian President to move to establish the Ogoniland Environmental Restoration Authority, which was recommended by the 2011 United Nations report.[54] The editorial noted that since oil theft costs Nigeria $3.65 billion per year, cracking down on oil theft would easily bring in enough to pay for the $1 billion initial budget.[55] The New York Times also pointed out that Shell, which just started deep-water production off Nigeria's coast, also has a responsibility to contribute to the $1 billion budget as well.[56]

---

[48] Id.
[49] Id.
[50] Id.
[51] Id.
[52] Id.
[53] Id.
[54] Id.
[55] Id.
[56] Oil's Devastating Legacy in Nigeria, By the Editorial Board, New York Times, (Aug. 14, 2014) http://www.nytimes.com/2014/08/15/opinion/oils-devastating-legacy-in-nigeria.html?emc=edit_ty_20140814&nl=opinion&nlid=55298393&_r=3 (last accessed on September 17, 2014).

A study was conducted by Enemugwem J.H., of the Department of History and Diplomatic Studies, Faculty of Humanities, University of Port Harcourt, Port Harcourt, Rivers State, Nigeria, on the effect of oil pollution on the people of Eastern Obolo (Andoni).[57] The findings of this study is reflective of the effects of oil pollution on the Niger Delta or oil producing communities of Nigeria as a whole. The Eastern Obolo (Andoni) people are a segment of the Obolo (Andoni) group that occupies the extreme corner of the Eastern Niger Delta.[58] As such, the Obolo (Andoni) are bounded by the Rio Real estuary in the west and the Cross River estuary in the east.[59] On their north and south are the Ogoni, the Ibibio and the Atlantic Ocean.[60] Because Eastern Obolo is located between the Imo and the Kwa Ibo rivers estuaries, their area of study is politically administered by the government of Akwa Ibom State of Nigeria.[61] Their kinsfolk of Western Obolo are in Rivers State with the Imo river estuary as the boundary point for Rivers and Akwa Ibom States.[62]

Enemugwem J.H in his study referred to the work of Fimsco Surveys (2002) which confirmed that Eastern Obolo ecosystem was rich in biodiversity and wildlife population before the commencement of oil exploration.[63] The dense rain forest and the transitory nature of the mangroves and saline water environment made the area a breeding ground for various species of fish and other marine lives, animals and plants.[64]

When the ancestors of the Eastern Obolo people led by Ede migrated into the area from Western Obolo over 300 years ago, they met and enjoyed a functional environment of unpolluted air, unpolluted water

---

[57] See. Enemugwem J.H., Oil Pollution and Eastern Obolo Human Ecology, 1957-2007, African Research Review Vol. 3 (1) (2009), Pp. 136-151, at 136 http://www.ajol.info/index.php/afrrev/article/viewFile/43561/27084 (last accessed September 12th 2014), ISSN 1994-9057 (Print), ISSN 2070-0083 (Online).

[58] Id. at 136.

[59] Id at 136-137.

[60] Id at 137.

[61] Id.

[62] Id.

[63] Id. at 137.

[64] Id.

and unpolluted land (Enemugwem 2000).[65] Water and land provided the artery for their economic development and transportation while the air they breathed was full of life for healthy living.[66] The water-laced environment bisected by a labyrinth of creeks and rivers of the mangrove ecosystem made fishing, trading, and salt making from saline water the economies of the people.[67] As soon as petroleum was discovered in the area in 1957, Shell Petroleum Development Company (SPDC) established their oil fields.[68] Later, Exxon Mobil and Elf, now Total, joined in the exploration and exploitation of the area.[69] Their activities heralded a new era of a polluted ecosystem.[70]

One of the areas Enemugwem J.H focused on is how oil exploitation activities silted up canals and estuaries in that area. Prior to oil prospecting, there were four viable estuaries in Eastern Obolo which link the wide continental shelf.[71] These estuaries were the mouths of the Imo, Obianga, Okwaan-Obolo and Okoroete-Iko rivers.[72] Together with the canals and the creek routes, like the Okoroete-Ibeno route, they linked the area with their neighboring communities.[73] These coastal waterways to the South Atlantic Sea were the means of the sandy beach ridges, the inter-tidal muddy mangrove swamps and labyrinths of saline rivers that became the topography of Eastern Obolo.[74] They also provided natural habitats to seafood.[75]

The study noted that today, these estuaries and canals are blocked due to the activities of the oil industries.[76] The study noted that it is not surprising that it leads to marine erosion.[77] It noted that as a result of these Eastern Obolo settlements, coastal banks are gradually

---

[65] Id. at 137.
[66] Id.
[67] Id.
[68] Id.
[69] Id. at 137.
[70] Id.
[71] Id. at 139.
[72] Id.
[73] Id.
[74] Id. at 139.
[75] Id.
[76] Id. at 139.
[77] Id.

eroding away.[78] The study named Okoroete Town, Elekokpoon, Emenoke I and II, Obianga, Ikonta and Iwofe as communities or settlements that are already eroding away.[79]

According to the study, in 1997, both Mobil and the Nigerian National Petroleum Corporation (NNPC) jointly sponsored an Environmental Impact Assessment to ascertain the effect of Mobil's Yoho Project on the host communities.[80] Eastern Obolo was in the report as likely to be negatively impacted.[81] In 1998, the same Mobil and NNPC engaged a firm, Unilag Consult, to assess the impact of their proposed expansion of the Qua Iboe Terminal.[82] The report submitted mentioned Ibeno, Eastern Obolo and Mbo Local Government Areas on the Akwa Ibom State coastline as likely to have their flora and fauna retarded.[83] As will be seen from further discussions in Chapter Three, the disregard of these Environmental Impact Assessments was a costly environmental misstep because there have been major oil spills from these Exxon Mobil oil facilities in 2010 and 2012, which rank among the worst oil spills in the history of oil spills in Nigeria's oil producing communities.

The study acknowledges that no sooner than the above projects were completed, the leakage of pipes and oil spillages from it and others rendered ponds, rivers, creeks and lands in Eastern Obolo polluted.[84] In fact, the oil spillages of January 1998 and November 2000 were worse in Eastern Obolo.[85] Thousands of barrels of Qua Iboe Light crude oil produced by Exxon Mobil were spilled into Eastern Obolo, Ibeno and Mbo Local Government Areas.[86] Before then oil spills in the Niger Delta had been affecting Eastern Obolo (Andoni) and they have had their own share of past oil spills.[87]

---

[78] Id.
[79] Id. at 139.
[80] Id.
[81] Id.
[82] Id. at 139.
[83] Id.
[84] Id. at 139.
[85] Id.
[86] Id.
[87] Id.

The study explained that when you take the adverse effects into consideration, the foremost is health hazard.[88] It noted that gas flare causes intense heat or physiological disorder.[89] Acid rains from gas flaring causes heat rashes, respiratory problems, skin cancer and bronchial pains.[90] All of these and cholera outbreaks occurred in Eastern Obolo between 1957 and 2007.[91] The study found that cholera outbreak owes its occurrence to pollution of streams which were the source of drinking water.[92] Another is cancer and stroke that were virtually unknown in the area before oil exploration but became real due to incessant oil spillages.[93] This study referred to an Ashton-Jones (1998) study that found that the Niger Delta region, which Eastern Obolo is a part, is exposed to fourteen other diseases due to oil exploration.[94] The lack of pipe-borne water makes streams and rivers their primary source of drinking water. This explains why they rely on water from streams and rivers and why they experience regular outbreaks of cholera.

The second impact of oil pollution noticed widely is poverty.[95] The study observed that the oil pollution and its poverty inducing effects is a reminder that in no way can humanity do without the natural resources of their environments.[96] Worst of all is the negative impact of the activities of the petroleum industry on the flora and fauna of the Eastern Obolo mangrove ecosystem.[97] The study found that oil pollution damaged the existence of viable plants and animals.[98] Not the least is damaging the ecology of the coral reefs.[99]

The study found that all the rivers, creeks and the estuaries of the Imo, Obianga, Okwaan-Obolo and Iko that were promoting the

---

[88] Id at 140.
[89] Id.
[90] Id. at 140.
[91] Id.
[92] Id. at 140.
[93] Id.
[94] Id. at 140.
[95] Id.
[96] Id.
[97] Id. at 140.
[98] Id.
[99] Id.

Eastern Obolo mangrove ecosystem were polluted.[100] Their economies of fishing, farming and salt making are no longer yielding good harvest due to oil pollution that reduces fish catch per-effort.[101] In recent times to get fish, the people go after the fishing trawlers in the deep sea, and buy the rotten and smaller fish and shrimp for resale.[102] Although it is their means of livelihood, going after it is dangerous.[103] Almost on weekly basis, two or three out of five persons in speed boats lose their lives while trying to buy fish from trawlers on the deep high sea.[104] The study found that this placed the people of Eastern Obolo (Andoni) under starvation as very small quantities of fish and sea animals enter the rivers and creeks from the South Atlantic Ocean due to the silting up of the estuaries.[105]

The poverty of the Eastern Obolo people increases as they cannot farm either.[106] The farmers experience deforestation that leads to loss of food sources because of the activities of the oil companies. Secondly, crops planted in oil polluted grounds absorb the oil and get destroyed.[107] Before oil exploration commenced, the indigenous food plants that serviced the economy and health of the people included bitter leaf, pepper, wild mango, cassava, plantain, cocoyam, water yam, tree leaf yam and yam.[108] The study referred to the oral account of Chief Daniel Ichen which emphasized that their absence, as well as fruits, spices and medicinal herbs, increased the people's poverty.[109] Lack of timbers such as iroko, mahogany, iron wood and mangrove trees that characterized the people's formerly flourishing timber export trade but destroyed by the oil wastes also increased their poverty level.[110] By virtue of these state of affairs the people are also denied their hunting, carving and craft industries.[111] Though it impoverished them, it also impoverished other Nigerians at the limits

---

[100] Id.at 140.
[101] Id.
[102] Id.
[103] Id.
[104] Id.
[105] Id. at 140.
[106] Id.
[107] Id.
[108] Id. at 140-141.
[109] Id. at 141.
[110] Id.
[111] Id.

of the Eastern Delta Rivers and creeks whose economies were serviced through the Eastern Obolo long distance trade.[112] This has increased unemployment and youth restiveness, not only in the area of study but also in the neighboring parts of the Niger Delta in general.[113]

The Enemugwem J.H study also found that the third adverse effects of the oil pollution in the Eastern Obolo ecosystem are food contamination and lack of security of life. It referenced a study by Onosode in 1998 which found that food contamination comes from pathogens, cyanide toxicity, mycotoxins and hydrocarbon contamination inflicted by the crude oil industries,[114] with the concomitant effect of short life span in Eastern Obolo. The study found that this has prompted migration of the Eastern Obolo people to Calabar, James Town, the Bakassi Peninsula and Rio del Rey in the Cameroons for safety.[115] Others migrate from Escravos to Badagry and the Lagos Lagoon and do their fishing and trading there.[116]

The study found that the cultural, archeological and historical sites and centers of the Eastern Obolo people have been desecrated by the effects of oil pollution and oil exploitation.[117] Eastern Obolo Local Government Area that was rich in historical and cultural heritage is now culturally impoverished due to oil fields and pipelines that traversed the area.[118] Their early settlements and cultural centers created many centuries ago on their migratory routes from Western Obolo (Andoni) to their present abodes have all been traversed by oil wells and pipelines.[119] The study outlines eleven settlements that used to be their cultural sites and burial grounds which today are "no-go areas" for the custodians of these cultural, historical and archaeological sites.[120] They are now in the right of way of the oil

---

[112] Id. at 141
[113] Id. at 141.
[114] Id.
[115] Id. at 141.
[116] Id.
[117] Id. at 141.
[118] Id.
[119] Id.
[120] Id. at 141.

fields and pipelines.[121] This destroyed the cultural sites that were in the land and creeks of Eastern Obolo.[122] The decay in social values, increase in social vices, loss of cultural sites and relics are synonymous with Eastern Obolo.[123] As a result, the community's social structure is under threat.[124]

2. Friction among the Key Players in Oil Producing Communities

Oil has been the driving force of conflicts between the oil communities and the oil companies on the one hand, and the oil communities and the government on the other hand. For instance, in the oil producing village of Oloibiri where the multinational oil company, Shell first struck oil in 1956, the people have continued to suffer colossal environmental despoliation and severe economic neglect (like lack of schools, roads, hospitals, pipe-borne water, electricity, and unemployment), even though they produce a large chunk of the oil, which sustains the Nigerian federation.[125] This perceived neglect has engendered protracted unrest in the Niger Delta region which crystallized into intractable crises for law enforcement authorities and frustrated oil and gas investors and their employees because it almost shut down oil production activities between 2005 and 2010 cutting production by 50%.

Due to the over-dependence of the Nigerian economy on oil, the government tends to be over-protective of the energy sector. For instance, the Oil Pipelines Act[126] imposes penalties on any person who willfully hinders or obstructs any licensees from entering or taking possession or using any land comprised in the license or without lawful authority interferes with or causes damage to any oil

[121] Id.
[122] Id.
[123] Id. at 141.
[124] Id.
[125] Environmental Rights Action. Environmental Testimonies #12. Dateline: Yenagoa, January 6, 1999 Subject: War and Terror in Ijawland, http://www.essentialaction.org/shell/era/eraEnvTest12.html (last accessed August 2, 2014).
[126] Cap 338 LFN 1990.

pipeline. The Petroleum Production and Distribution Anti-Sabotage Act 1975[127] prescribes more severe penalties. The Act creates the offense of sabotage in respect of willful acts calculated to disrupt or interfere with the distribution of petroleum products. Persons found guilty of the offense of sabotage are liable to death sentences or to imprisonment for 21 years. A stricter penalty of death by firing squad was provided under section 6(2) (e) of the Special Tribunal (Miscellaneous offenses) Decree No. 20 of 1984,[128] which provided that "any person who willfully or maliciously obstructs, damages, destroys or otherwise tampers or interferes with the free flow of any crude or refined petroleum product through an oil pipeline shall upon conviction be liable to suffer 'death by the firing squad." In 1999 this section was deleted in an amendment of the law and the title of the law was changed to Miscellaneous Offences Decree 1984 and the functions of the Tribunal and the pending cases with the Tribunals were transferred to the Federal High Court.[129]

Government regulators have given the oil companies unregulated freedom, and have persistently refused to enforce the subsisting meager environmental regimes. It has been alleged that the close collaboration between the government and the oil companies in the suppression of the protests of the Niger Delta people makes it difficult to distinguish between the two. It has been documented that oil companies like the Royal Dutch Shell Group allegedly provided money, weapons and logistical support to the Nigerian military, including the vehicles and ammunition used in the raids of villages in the Delta Region in the 1990s.[130] Shell has also been accused of having procured at least some of these attacks, participated in the fabrication of murder charges, and bribed witnesses to give false testimony[131] even though Shell has consistently denied these accusations.[132]

[127] Cap 353. Volume XX, LFN 1990.
[128] Cap 410. Volume XXII, LFN 1990.
[129] Schedule 1, Part 1, Tribunals (Certain Consequential Amendments) Decree No 62 of 1999, Laws of the Federation of Nigeria.
[130] See Craig Forcese, ATCA'S Achilles Heel: Corporate Complicity, International Law and the Alien Tort Claims Act, 26 Yale J. Int'l L. 487, 490 (Summer 2001).
[131] Id. at 490.
[132] Id.

Problems between oil companies and their host communities cause the latter to sometimes engage in the sabotage of oil pipelines and crude oil thefts which contributes to 28% of oil spills in the Niger Delta.[133] To mitigate this, the concept of the Petroleum Host Communities Fund (PHCF) was included in a 2012 Bill, known as the "Petroleum Industry Bill (PIB)" which was presented by the executive arm of the Federal Government of Nigeria to the Nigerian National Assembly.[134]The Petroleum Host Community Fund (PHC Fund) is established under sections 116 to 118 of the PIB and is to be utilized for the development of the economic and social infrastructure of the communities within petroleum producing areas.[135] The concept emanated from the Senate version of the PIB in the course of its work after Public Hearings.[136] Within the Senate version of the Bill, it was called the Petroleum Producing Communities Fund.[137]

The suggested source of funding for the PHC Fund shall consist of a monthly remittance of 10% of its net profits derived by every petroleum producing company from upstream petroleum operations in onshore areas, offshore and shallow waters, which shall be made directly into the PHC Fund.'[138] 10% of profits derived from upstream petroleum operations in deep water areas shall also be paid into the Fund, for the benefit of the 'producing littoral states.'[139] These are

---

[133] By Dele Ogbodo, Niger Delta Oil Spills: Senate Takes the Gauntlet, Moves to Amend NOSDRA Act 2006, This Day Newspaper, This Day Live, (4 November 2012) http://www.thisdaylive.com/articles/n-delta-oil-spills-senate-takes-the-gauntlet-moves-to-amend-nosdra-act-2006/129571/ (last accessed September 7, 2014).

[134] NEITI Position on the Petroleum Industry Bill 2012, p 37, Nigeria Extractive Industry Transparency Initiative, The Presidency (2013) http://neiti.org.ng/sites/default/files/press-release/uploads/neiti-position-final.pdf (last visited on October 5, 2014).

[135] See id at 37, see also section 117 of the Senate version of the PIB.

[136] See id at 37.

[137] Id. at 37.

[138] Id.

[139] See id at 37, see also section 118 of the Senate version of the PIB, see also, An Analysis of the Nigerian Petroleum Industry Bill 2012, Vol 1, By Samuel Diminas, p 7, footnotes 1-3, Wespaq (May 2013) http://www.westpaq.com/wp-content/uploads/2013/05/An-Analysis-of-the-Nigerian-Petroleum-Industry-Bill-2012_WESTPAQ_v1_FINAL.pdf (last accessed October 5, 2014) where net profit for the purpose of Section 118, is defined as "adjusted profit, less royalty,

tax deductible amounts and will 'constitute a credit to its total fiscal rent obligations as defined in the PIB.'[140] The PIB also provides that in the event of a sabotage of oil facilities and installations resulting in an oil spill, the cost of cleaning up the oil spill will be defrayed from the PHC Fund if the evidence available shows that an oil producing community is culpable in the sabotage.

An oil and gas industry expert and commentator Samuel Diminas opines that "the PHCF is likely to enhance peace and stability in the Niger Delta if the communities profit directly from production."[141] He believes that "an increase in production would result in an increase in funds to the PHCF's and vice versa," thereby forging and cementing a symbiotic relationship between the host communities and the producing companies.[142] According to him, "in this scenario, the benefit and loss of one affects the other."[143] Samuel Diminas states further that the "net effect of the PHCF is expected to be an increase in revenues for the government and the oil companies as a result of reduction in production disruptions."[144]

Samuel Diminas using Shell Petroleum Development Company (SPDC) as a case study found that Shell spent about $383 million on

---

allowable deductions and allowances, less Nigerian Hydrocarbon Tax, less companies' income tax. PIB 2012, Section 118 (2)." 'Shallow areas' is defined as "offshore production in shallow water," while 'Shallow water' is defined as "areas in the offshore of Nigeria up to and including a water depth of 200 meters. PIB 2012 Section 363. Interpretations." 'Deep-water' is defined as "areas offshore Nigeria with water depth in excess of 200 meters. PIB 2012, Section 363. Interpretations."

[140] See. NEITI Position on the Petroleum Industry Bill 2012, p 37, Nigeria Extractive Industry Transparency Initiative, The Presidency (2013) http://neiti.org.ng/sites/default/files/press-release/uploads/neiti-position-final.pdf (last visited on October 5, 2014).

[141] See. An Analysis of the Nigerian Petroleum Industry Bill 2012, Vol 1, By Samuel Diminas, p 7, Wespaq (May 2013) http://www.westpaq.com/wp-content/uploads/2013/05/An-Analysis-of-the-Nigerian-Petroleum-Industry-Bill-2012_WESTPAQ_v1_FINAL.pdf (last accessed October 5, 2014).

[142] Id at 7.

[143] Id.

[144] See. An Analysis of the Nigerian Petroleum Industry Bill 2012, Vol 1, By Samuel Diminas, p 7, Wespaq (May 2013) http://www.westpaq.com/wp-content/uploads/2013/05/An-Analysis-of-the-Nigerian-Petroleum-Industry-Bill-2012_WESTPAQ_v1_FINAL.pdf (last accessed October 5, 2014).

security between 2007 and 2009 in Nigeria.[145] His research of Shell's accounting books showed that in 2008 alone, Shell expended more on
security in the Delta than in the Americas, European Union (EU) and Russia combined.[146] Samuel Diminas inferred from this discovery that enhanced peace and stability would significantly reduce security cost for oil producing companies while also engendering stable production in the Niger Delta.[147] He observed that while it may be conceded "that the PHCF would not be a silver bullet to eliminate all security or community/oil and gas company dispute in the Niger Delta, it would be a positive step towards addressing some level of dissatisfaction felt by host communities."[148]

Samuel Diminas in his analysis supported his argument with the example of a company that implemented a community profit participation program with its host community and is reaping the benefits of doing so. His model or example is the "Indorama Eleme Petrochemical Ltd (IEPL), located in Port Harcourt, Rivers state, Nigeria, which was a 100% subsidiary of Nigerian Government-owned Nigerian National Petroleum Corporation (NNPC) with the name Eleme Petrochemicals Company Limited (EPCL)."[149] He stated that "The Indorama Group acquired the EPCL under the 2006 privatization program in Nigeria."[150] His research reveals that Indorama Eleme Petrochemicals operates a model in which communities have a 7.5 % Equity Share Partnership.[151] His examination of the financial records of the company in the last few years shows that this 7.5% Equity Share has translated into an annual dividend of more than N4 billion per annum for IEPL's six host communities.[152] Samuel Diminas observed that "with this model, the IEPL has gone on to be a very successful company, recording achievements of smooth and stable operations, enhanced production capacities, winning several global awards and certifications and has

[145] Id at 8.
[146] Id. at 8.
[147] Id.
[148] Id. at 8.
[149] Id. at 8.
[150] Id.
[151] Id. at 8.
[152] Id.

become a successful model of Nigeria's Privatization Program.[153] Samuel Diminas noted that IEPL signed a Project Financing Package for US$ 1.2 Billion for a Greenfield Urea Fertilizer Plant in the same host community.[154]

It is not certain if the PIB and its PHC Fund provision will become law because of the enormous opposition it faces from the oil companies and certain states of the Nigerian Federation which believe that certain provisions of the PIB and the PHC Fund provision are unnecessary and could engender divestment by oil companies in Nigeria's Upstream Oil sector or reduce the allocation of the oil revenue to their respective states.[155] This much was made known at a Public hearing on the PIB hosted by the upper legislative chamber of Nigeria, the Senate in 2013.[156]

If the PIB is passed into law in Nigeria and the provisions on the PHC Fund is retained in the legislation, it could have a significant effect on the percentage of oil spills caused by sabotage of oil facilities by disgruntled host communities, provided proper mechanisms and guidelines are put in place to ensure that the funds are judiciously managed.[157]

---

[153] Id. at 8.
[154] Id.
[155] PIB, a Killer, Say IOCs, by Omololu Ogunmade and Chineme Okafor, (July 19, 2013), This Day Newspaper, This Day Live, http://www.thisdaylive.com/articles/pib-a-killer-say-iocs/153774/ (last updated October 5, 2014)
[156] Id.
[157] See. NEITI Position on the Petroleum Industry Bill 2012, p 37, Nigeria Extractive Industry Transparency Initiative, The Presidency (2013) http://neiti.org.ng/sites/default/files/press-release/uploads/neiti-position-final.pdf (last visited on October 5, 2014) (arguing that mode of disbursement is not provided for and there is no structure, and no detailed functions and objectives. NEITI is concerned that the Bill has no governance rules, and fails to state how the PHC Fund shall be administered. Instead, the Minister is mandated to make regulations on entitlement, governance and management. No time period is given for the Minister to make these regulations, leaving open the possibility that the Fund could end up functioning in the absence of clearly defined procedures).

CHAPTER TWO

1. The Statutory and Regulatory Regimes Applicable

In the 1980s, a series of environmental disasters forced the government to promulgate *albeit ex post facto*, a set of national environmental standards.[158] The three documents that embodied the Nigerian environmental policy were The National Policy on The Environment, The Federal Environmental Protection Agency Decree (1988), and the Harmful Waste (Special Criminal Provisions) Decree of 1988. The Harmful Waste (Special Criminal Provisions) Act[159] was the only document that dealt mainly with hazardous and toxic wastes. The dumping by an Italian firm of toxic waste in Nigeria in 1988 was the catalyst the government needed to enact these legislations.[160]

Nigeria also has a number of incidental provisions in various statute books dealing with oil pollution. These include The Petroleum Act (1969),[161] The Petroleum (Drilling and Production) Regulation,[162] Mineral Oils (safety) Regulations,[163] Associated Gas Re-Injection (Amendment) Decree,[164] Oil in Navigable Waters Act, 1968.[165] The Oil in Navigable Waters Act is solely devoted to oil pollution of waters but it is severely restricted and provides for a myriad of very liberal defenses.[166]

---

[158] See. Pita Agbese. Nigeria's Environment: Crises, Consequences and Responses in Environmental Policies in The Third World: A Comparative Analysis. 125 (O.P. Dwivedi & Dhirendran K Vajpeyi eds., 1995).
[159] Act No. 42 of 1988, Cap H1 L.F.N. 2004.
[160] See. Nigeria Waste Imports from Italy (NIGERIA), Case Number 52, http://www1.american.edu/ted/nigeria.htm (last accessed, July 29, 2014)
[161] CAP 350 LFN 1990.
[162] Cap 350 LFN 1990.
[163] Enacted in Legal Notice 69 of 1968.
[164] Cap 350 LFN Schedule 4.
[165] Decree No.4 of 1968, Cap 337 LFN 1990.
[166] Cap 337 LFN 1990.

Other legislations include Oil Pipelines Act[167] and the Criminal Code.[168] Common law and international law also applies however, the Federal Environmental Protection Agency Act 1988 (hereinafter referred to as FEPA) was the most comprehensive environmental legislation passed in Nigeria as of the time it was passed.[169] We shall consequently look into the FEPA Act and other relevant laws, both domestic and international, as a guide to examining the normative effectiveness or otherwise of Nigerian statutes in preventing and remedying oil pollution in the Niger Delta region.

The more recent legislations which will also be discussed include the National Environmental Standards and Regulations Enforcement Agency (NASREA) Act[170] and the National Oil Spill Detection Response Agency Establishment Act (NOSDRA).[171]

---

[167] See. Decree No. 31. 1956, See, also, Ambrose O.O. Ekpu, Environmental Impact of Oil on Water: A Comparative Overview of the Law and Policy in the United States and Nigeria, 24 Denv. J. Int'l L. & Pol'y at 83.

[168] Cap 77, Volume V. LFN 1990.

[169] Cap 131, Volume VIII. LFN 1990.

[170] NASREA Act No. 25 of 2007, Cap N164 LFN 2007.

[171] NOSDRA Act, Cap 157 LFN 2006.

CHAPTER THREE

1. THE KEY NORMATIVE ISSUES AT STAKE.

In the examination of each normative concept, the approach will be one of identifying the existing legal framework, problems associated with each, and using the U.S. as model for reform.

2. A. I. STANDING: THE CITIZENS AND NON-GOVERNMENTAL ORGANIZATION'S RIGHT TO SUE

The citizen suit provisions in Federal environmental statutes shift the power of enforcement discretion from the Executive branch to private citizens, allowing them to become "private attorney generals."[172] It is therefore one of the arsenals of an injured plaintiff in the US to compel a government agency to enforce the environmental laws in the statute books. It often occurs when there is a manifestation of reluctance on the part of the executive in the enforcement of environmental laws. Unfortunately in Nigeria, the lack of any mechanism for private enforcement of the statutes and regulations compounds the problem of non-enforcement by the public agencies.[173]

The non-inclusion of citizen suits in Nigerian environmental laws is due to the desire to attract investment to the oil industry and to prevent any interruption in the exploitation, production, distribution and transportation of oil in Nigeria, taking into cognizance the fact that over 85% of Nigeria's revenue is derived from oil. This is a sharp contrast to the US where nearly every major federal environmental legislation have provisions for citizen suits.[174] A legal commentator articulated the US position on citizen suits, when she said:

---

[172] See Natalie Bussan: All Bark and No Bite: Citizen Suits After Steel Company V. Cbe, 6 Wis. Envtl. L. J. 195, 196 (Summer 1999).

[173] See. id at 196.

[174] Ambrose 0.0. Ekpu, Environmental Impact of Oil on Water: A Comparative Overview of the Law and Policy in the United States and Nigeria, 24 Denv. J. Int'l L. & Pol'y 55, 99 (Fall 1995).

"Congress first enacted citizen suit provisions in the early 1970's in both the Clean Air Act and the Clean Water Act. The following environmental statutes have citizen suit provisions nearly identical to those of the Clean Air Act and Clean Water Act: Toxic Substances Control Act; Endangered Species Act; Surface Mining Control and Reclamation Act; Marine Protection, Research and Sanctuaries Act; Safe Drinking Water Act; Noise Control Act; Solid Waste Disposal Act; Comprehensive Environmental Response, Compensation, and Liability Act; and the Emergency Planning and Community Right to Know Act. Congress envisioned that suits brought by citizens would ensure good environmental industry standards and government enforcement."[175]

2. A. II. Private Causes of Action

A statement that captures the challenge of balancing the need to aggressively protect the environment with that of economic development and the need for reform especially with regard to the situation in Nigeria is that of former U.S. President Nixon, when he said:

"The basic causes of our environmental troubles are complex and deeply imbedded. They include: our past tendency to emphasize quantitative growth at the expense of qualitative growth, the failure of our economy to provide full accounting for the social costs of environmental pollution; the failure to take environmental factors into account as normal and necessary part of our planning and decision making, the inadequacy of our institutions for dealing with problems that cut across traditional political boundaries; our dependence on conveniences, without regard for their impact on the environment; and more fundamentally, our failure to perceive the environment as a totality and to understand and to recognize the fundamental interdependence of all parts, including man himself."[176]

Private causes of action allow injured citizens to go beyond the normal elements of citizen suits, which is limited to compelling the enforcement agencies to do their job. Here, the injured individual would seek compensatory damages for the injuries sustained. This might include damage to property, loss of subsistence use of natural

---

[175] Id. at 99.

[176] See. Olubunmi Olanrewaju Awoyemi, Ph.D, The Anatomy of United States' Oil Pollution Act of 1990, M.O. Awoyemi & Co. Independent Law Publishing (2013) (citing Ex- President Nixon's message to the U.S Congress, The First Annual Report of the Council on Environmental Quality at 7).

resources which includes the domestic use of water and fishing for food.

In Nigeria, by contrast, the absence as of September 2014 of statutory provisions permitting private rights of action has left the common law as the only refuge for victims of oil pollution who seek judicial remedies.[177] Due to the numerous drawbacks associated with common law tort actions, the victims' chances of recovering any substantial and meaningful remedy are slim.[178] The claimants are thus constrained to accept whatever compensation is offered to them by the polluting oil companies, no matter how grossly and ostensibly inadequate those offers might be.[179] The Nigerian courts make the alternative option of litigation even more unattractive because of the paltry awards they give in the few cases that succeed.[180] For instance, in Mon v. Shell BP Petroleum Development Company of Nigeria Ltd.,[181] the court found that the spillage from the defendant's pipelines caused enormous damage to the plaintiffs' fish pond but awarded only two hundred naira (equivalent to $1.21) as damages for the plaintiffs' loss. In another case, Nweke v. Nigerian Agip Oil Company Ltd.,[182] the court merely awarded the exact amount initially offered by the defendant but rejected earlier by the plaintiffs.

In 2003, the Federal High Court, Lagos, ordered oil giant Exxon Mobil Corp. to pay nearly $10 million in damages to three Niger Delta oil producing communities for a pipeline oil spill that occurred in 1998.[183] Exxon Mobil as of 2003 produced about 800,000 barrels

---

[177] See Natalie Bussan: All Bark And No Bite: Citizen Suits After Steel Company v. Cbe, 6 Wis. Envtl. L.J. at 196- 197.

[178] Ambrose O.O. Ekpu. Environmental Impact of Oil on Water: A Comparative Overview of the Law and Policy in the United States and Nigeria, 24 Denv. J. Int'l L. & Pol'y at 100.

[179] Id.

[180] Id.

[181] See id. at 100 (citing, Mon v. Shell BP Petroleum Development Company of Nigeria Ltd., (1970-72) 1 R.S.L.R. at 71).

[182] See id. at 100 (citing (1996) 9-10 S.C. 101).

[183] See. Cable News Network, World News: Exxon Mobil fined $10 million for Nigeria oil spill, (Wednesday, December 10, 2003), http://www.cnn.com/2003/WORLD/africa/12/08/exxon.fine.ap/ (Last accessed September 12, 2004 and currently archived and no longer on line)), See, also, Fin 24 Archives, ExxonMobil Ordered to pay $10m,

daily in Nigeria and is the second-largest operator in Nigeria after Royal Dutch Shell Group.[184] The Irving, Texas-based company's local subsidiary, Mobil Producing Nigeria Unlimited, immediately after the judgment said it would appeal the decision ordering it to pay $9.6 million to the towns of Bonny, Brass and Andoni.[185] The named Niger Delta towns are near the site of the January 1998 pipeline rupture that spilled between 40,000 and 100,000 barrels of crude into the region's river and marshlands.[186] Justice Abdullahi Mustapha of the Federal High Court decided that the spill caused environmental damage to the three communities.[187] Unfortunately, the company spokesman Udom Inoyo claimed "there was no discernible adverse effect on the people and the environment."[188] In early 2004, Exxon Mobil appealed the decision with the aim of reducing the amount awarded.[189]

Some commentators pointed out the dim chances of getting significant compensation through litigation based on the common law.[190] These commentators pointed out that interviews with community leaders and activist groups showed a general lack of awareness of the value and effectiveness of court actions.[191] They noted that even though this is gradually changing, many activists and leaders profess little confidence in the ability of the current court system to assist them.[192]They said that these activists claimed that oil companies usually respond to litigation with continuous, unending appeals, ensuring that litigants do not benefit from their legal

---

http://www.fin24.com/Companies/ExxonMobil-ordered-to-pay-10m-20031208 (last accessed September 12th, 2014).

[184] See. Id.

[185] Id.

[186] Id.

[187] Id

[188] Id.

[189] Id.

[190] See. Emeka Duruigbo, Owen Wozniak, and Michelle Leighton, Oil Development in Nigeria: A critical investigation of Chevron Corporation's performance in the Niger River Delta, CALIFORNIA GLOBAL CORPORATE ACCOUNTABILITY PROJECT, The Nautilus Institute for Security and Sustainable Development, p 5 (2001).

[191] Id. at 5.

[192] Id at 5-6.

victory.[193] They also noted that the cost of suing the government or oil companies makes it very difficult for many individuals and communities, thereby making the right to private enforcement of environmental laws virtually non-existent in Nigeria.[194] The commentators concluded that until some mechanism for funding environmental and human rights litigation is established, high costs will continue to prevent many Nigerians from exercising their rights.[195] So, while the nearly $10m award is the highest in Nigeria's history, it may not stand on appeal, and if it does stand, it may take many years to reach a resolution on the matter, and many more years to enforce the judgment. As of September 2014, there is no indication that the judgment was upheld or that the case has been disposed of by the Appellate Court system in Nigeria despite the fact that the Federal High Court judgment was delivered 11 years ago.

A punitive damage award of $4.5 billion by a United States District Court that was later reduced by an appellate court to $2.5b and later to $507.5 million in the Exxon Valdez oil spill case in the United States underlines the effectiveness and versatility of US common law remedies for oil pollution, in sharp contrast to the ineffectiveness of the common law remedies in Nigeria's oil pollution litigation.[196] The paltry awards that are made by Nigerian courts in suits based on common law indicates that there is need for a specific statutory provision that allows for private causes of action in oil pollution cases in Nigeria. And the statute should include generous damages provisions, including punitive damages to protect the victims of oil pollution.

Statutory intervention is critical because ExxonMobil and other multinational oil companies have imbibed a culture of impunity as far as the Niger Delta environment is concerned. In 2012, an oil spill at an ExxonMobil facility offshore from the Niger Delta spread at least 20 miles from its source, coating waters used by fishermen in a

---

[193] Id. at 6.
[194] Id.
[195] Id. at 6.
[196] See. Exxon Valdez Oil Spill, Litigation and Clean-up Costs, https://en.wikipedia.org/wiki/Exxon_Valdez_oil_spill (last accessed August 20th, 2014).

film of sludge.[197] A Reuters reporter visiting several parts of Akwa Ibom state saw a rainbow-tinted oil slick stretching for 20 miles from a pipeline that Exxon had shut down because of a leak a week earlier.[198] Mark Ward, the Managing Director of ExxonMobil's local unit, said a clean-up had been mobilized, and he apologized to affected communities for the spill.[199]

Exxon Mobil announced some days earlier that it had shut a pipeline off the coast of Akwa Ibom state after an oil leak whose cause was unknown.[200] "This is the worst spill in this community since Exxon started its operations in the area," said Edet Asuquo, 40, a fisherman in the Mkpanak community, as women scooped oil into buckets.[201] In some marshy areas, plants were poking out of the slick, not yet dead but blackened by the oil.[202] "The fishermen cannot fish any longer and have no alternative means of survival," Asuquo said.[203]

"Mobil Producing Nigeria (MPN) regrets this incident. Our teams are being mobilized to clean up the area," Ward said in a statement emailed to Reuters.[204] "We apologize for the inconveniences that it has caused."[205]

One fisherman described noticing a large quantity of oil on the surface of the sea and all over the beach some days earlier, adding that the company has since sprayed chemicals in the water, which was helping to disperse it.[206] It was the second major oil spill near Exxon facilities in three months.[207] At the end of August 2012, an oil spill left a slick running for miles along the coast.[208] Reuters noted

---

[197] ExxonMobil Oil Spill Ravages Akwa Ibom, Information Nigeria, (November 18, 2012) http://www.informationng.com/2012/11/exxonmobil-oil-spill-ravages-akwa-ibom.html (last accessed on September 12, 2014).
[198] Id.
[199] Id.
[200] Id.
[201] Id.
[202] Id.
[203] Id.
[204] Id.
[205] Id.
[206] Id.
[207] Id.
[208] Id.

that oil spills are common in Nigeria, where enforcement of environmental regulations is lax.[209]

As discussed earlier, the UNEP report in August of 2011 criticized the government and multinational oil firms for 50 years of oil pollution that has devastated the Ogoni land region of Rivers State.[210] "Our prayers are for tough punishment on the oil companies operating in the Niger Delta," said Inyang Ekong, the secretary of the Fishermen's Association, as the car he was in swept past oil washing up onto beaches in an area called Ibeno.[211]

Critics observed that Oil Major BP Plc around the time of the ExxonMobil Niger Delta Oil Spill being discussed occurred agreed to pay $4.5 billion in penalties for spilling nearly 5 million barrels of oil into the Gulf of Mexico in 2010.[212] Despite thousands of barrels a year spilt by oil majors in Nigeria, none has ever been forced to make a financially significant settlement.[213]

Two years before the 2012 oil spill, there was an oil spill from the exact same ExxonMobil in the same area of the Niger Delta. Sahara Reporters' team of investigative reporters learnt that three reasons account for the recurrent oil spills from ExxonMobil's platforms at the Qua Iboe Terminal in Akwa Ibom State.[214]

Two oil industry monitors told Sahara Reporters' investigative correspondent that the first factor is ExxonMobil's total disregard of international industry standards for pipelines maintenance.[215] The second has to do with compromise and collusion between officials of oil multinationals and Nigerian government officials in charge of

---

[209] Id.
[210] Id.
[211] Id.
[212] Id.
[213] Id.
[214] ExxonMobil, Nigerian officials blamed for Akwa Ibom Oil Spills, Sahara Reporters, (June 29th 2010) http://saharareporters.com/2010/06/29/exxonmobil-nigerian-officials-blamed-akwa-ibom-spills (last accessed, September 12, 2014).
[215] Id.

regulating the oil industry's environmentally impacting activities and enforcing the environmental laws on the books.[216]

The third cause, in the words of one source, "is ExxonMobil's despicable practice of cutting corners in its exploration activities in Nigeria's Niger Delta region."[217]

ExxonMobil recorded the 2010 oil spill into the Atlantic Ocean near the Ibeno shoreline, the second such spill in a week.[218] The spillage happened following a rupture in the export hose of an oil vessel, NorthStar.[219] At the time, NorthStar was taking crude from the Yoho field, a floating storage and offloading vessel (FSO).[220]

Sahara Reporters stated that their sources disclosed that the pipelines which carry crude to the Qua Iboe Terminal are dilapidated and decrepit.[221] "ExxonMobil's refusal to replace these pipelines lead to these frequent oil spills from the Qua Iboe Terminal area," said one source.[222]

The same source described the Yoho vessel called NorthStar as "a huge piece of metal scrap that was expelled from Angola a few years ago."[223] Their investigation revealed that the Angolan government had driven the vessel out of their waters because the vessel is over 30 years old.[224] "Unfortunately, Nigerian officials who went to inspect the vessel where it was being refurbished approved it for use in Nigerian waters," said a source, adding that she suspects that hefty bribes exchanged hands.[225]

An environmental activist based in Port Harcourt told Sahara Reporters that he was dismayed to see ExxonMobil use the vessel "to

---

[216] Id.
[217] Id.
[218] Id.
[219] Id.
[220] Id.
[221] Id.
[222] Id.
[223] Id.
[224] Id.
[225] Id.

cause incalculable environmental harm in the Niger Delta."[226] He added: "The company is acting with impunity because there's nobody holding them to account.[227] Would they dare do the same thing in Europe or the US?"[228]

ExxonMobil officials tried to minimize the extent of the oil spill from the NorthStar.[229] "The company claimed that only two barrels of crude oil spilled into the Atlantic," said a source, "but that's falsehood."[230] The source said that export hoses would rupture only after showing signs of dilapidation over time.[231] They also said the ruptures suggested that corrupt or inept Nigerian officials had failed to conduct the periodic pressure tests mandated to check the integrity of hoses.[232] "The truth is that the Nigerian officials who have legal authority and obligation to monitor compliance with standards are often more interested in monitoring the slush of cash into their pockets," said an industry observer.[233]

One Nigerian employee said it is not the first time the export hose in Yoho failed, but that ExxonMobil was good at hiding the spill or issuing a denial whenever it happened."[234] He stated that Sahara Reporters' recent searchlights on the problem forced the company to start admitting spills, albeit reluctantly.[235]

A recent industry report indicted ExxonMobil for its use of the Yoho platform.[236] The report stated that "Deploying an Early Production Systems (EPS) on Yoho allows ExxonMobil to get to first oil 2 years earlier than a full floating production facility would allow in Nigeria."[237] According to the report, ExxonMobil's internal publications attest to the company's use of questionable methods to

---

226 Id.
227 Id.
228 Id.
229 Id.
230 Id.
231 Id.
232 Id.
233 Id.
234 Id.
235 Id.
236 Id.
237 Id.

shorten the process of crude production at the expense of the environment.[238] "There's no question that ExxonMobil took a shortcut to put in place a fast-track floating, production, storage and offloading (FPSO) vessel," said an environmental activist, adding, "that decision has become a disaster for the people and environment of Akwa Ibom state and the Niger Delta region in general."[239]

Unfortunately, on the 30th of June 2014, another oil spill from ExxonMobil, the operator of Qua Iboe Terminal, occurred again, affecting Nkpana; Inua Eyet Ikot and Esuk Ikim Ekeme communities in Ibeno Local Government Area of Akwa Ibom State.[240] The spill reportedly occurred when a thunderstorm caused a fire.[241] The amount of oil lost to the fire and spill had not been calculated at the time of the newspaper report. The Village Head of Iwuo Okpom, a community in Ibeno, Okon Akpanubong, urged ExxonMobil to begin clean up without delay.[242] He appealed to the Federal Government and other relevant agencies to come to the people's rescue.[243] The village head lamented that there had been series of oil spills since the company came on board, thus making the local communities lose confidence in ExxonMobil.[244] He complained that the spillage has extended to the ocean and to the coast communities. The Coordinator of Artisan Fishermen Association of Nigeria, John Etim, said fishermen are facing hardship because of the spill.[245]

---

[238] Id.
[239] Id.
[240] By Kazeem Ibrahym, Oil Spill in Akwa Ibom, July 1, 2014, The Nation Newspaper http://thenationonlineng.net/new/oil-spill-in-akwa-ibom/ (last accessed October 8, 2014)
[241] Id.
[242] Id.
[243] Id.
[244] By Bernard Tolani Dada, Oil Spillage Ravages 3 Communities In Akwa Ibom, June 30, 2014, Leadership Newspaper, http://leadership.ng/news/376520/oil-spillage-ravages-3-communities-akwa-ibom (last accessed October 8, 2014).
[245] By Kazeem Ibrahym, Oil Spill in Akwa Ibom, July 1, 2014, The Nation Newspaper http://thenationonlineng.net/new/oil-spill-in-akwa-ibom/ (last accessed October 8, 2014)

2. B. Public Participation in Environmental Regulation

Many multinational oil companies have been recording spills in Nigeria over which the voices of the local people have remained drowned in the noise of the oil rigs and gas flares. Unless the people and communities who have to live with environmental pollution are actively and meaningfully involved in the decision-making process, it is irrelevant as to whether environmental regulatory control is located at the Federal, State, or Local level.[246]

For too long, the voice of the public in environmental regulation, which is an essential part of democracy, has been tokenized, stifled, drowned out by industry, or otherwise ignored.[247] With increasing privatization, marketization, and decentralization of environmental decision-making, increased public participation is essential to achieving environmental justice.[248] True public participation and environmental justice cannot be realized until the communities that are impacted by environmental regulations have a voice in the process equal to that of regulated industry.[249] In other words the participation of potential victims of oil pollution in the drafting of statutes and regulations is crucial to the promulgation of fair environmental laws.

In the U.S., public outrage often provides the catalytic spark for the passage of Federal environmental legislation; environmental catastrophes and reports invoking visions of impending disaster create intense collective anxiety, assuaged only by seemingly "tough" legislation.[250] This is not the case in Nigeria, where public outcry has not engendered public participation. Meaningful and effective public participation has not been incorporated into the normal legislative and regulatory drafting process.

---

[246] Scott Kuhn, Regulation of Pollutants: Federal, State, And Local Expanding Public Participation Is Essential to Environmental Justice and the Democratic Decision making Process, 25 Ecology L.Q. 647 (1999).
[247] Id. at 647-648.
[248] Id. at 648.
[249] Id.
[250] Eileen Gauna, Case: The Environmental Justice Misfit: Public Participation And The Paradigm Paradox. 17 Stan. Envtl. L..J. 3, 4 (1998).

Due to the fore-going, the approach to public participation in the drafting of environmental statutes in the U.S can serve as a template for reform in Nigeria. In the U.S., public comments are normally required before an agency's regulations can finally become law. The stakeholders in industry groups whose activities impact the environment are allowed to make their views and concerns known to the crafters of the regulations, so as to ensure that the regulations are fair and enforceable. The potential victims of pollution (including NGOs who fight for their rights) are also allowed to do the same. This symbiosis and cross fertilization of often dissimilar ideas and concerns crystallize into regulations that are both fair to all, and enforceable.

In Nigeria the legislative and regulation drafting process is devoid of the aforementioned factors which make US laws fair and enforceable primarily because of the non-participation of potential victims. A lopsided participation of only the regulated oil industry is tantamount to giving the regulated industry the unfair advantage of more or less drafting the regulations themselves.

In the US for example, the Environmental Protection Agency (EPA) released the "Draft 2000 Public Involvement Policy" on December 28, 2000 and accepted public comments on the Policy through July 31, 2001.[251] The Policy which came into effect on June 6, 2003[252] provides guidance and direction to EPA officials on effective means to involve the public in its regulatory and program decisions.[253] The Draft Policy was developed based on recommendations in the "'Engaging the American People: A Review of EPA's Public Participation Policy and Regulations with Recommendations for Action" report.[254]

[251] 65 F.R . 82335 (2000).

[252] 68 F.R. 33946-33949 http://www.gpo.gov/fdsys/pkg/FR-2003-06-06/html/03-14325.htm> (last accessed September 19, 2014), see also http://www.gpo.gov/fdsys/pkg/FR-2003-06-06/pdf/03-14325.pdf (last accessed September 19, 2014.

[253] 65 F.R . 82335.

[254] Public Involvement Policy of the U.S. Environmental Protection Agency, p 1-2, May 2003 http://www.epa.gov/publicinvolvement/pdf/policy2003.pdf (last accessed on August 17, 2014).

The purposes of the Policy are to: strengthen EPA's commitment to early and meaningful public involvement: ensure that environmental decisions are made with an understanding of the interest and concerns of affected people and entities; promote the use of a wide variety of techniques to create opportunities for public involvement in agency decisions; and establish clear and effective procedures for conducting public involvement activities in EPA's decision-making processes.[255]

The policy applies to all EPA programs, including activities such as rulemaking for significant regulations, permit issuance or modification, selection of plans for cleanup of hazardous waste sites, and other significant policy decisions.[256] The policy does not replace public participation requirements established by existing laws or regulations, but supplements those requirements and enables the EPA to implement them in the most effective ways.[257]

The new Draft Policy is based on an earlier policy issued in 1981 that was never fully implemented.[258] The new Policy parallels the old one, except that it addresses many changes that have occurred since 1981. These include: EPA's additional responsibilities under new statutes, regulations and Executive Orders; new and expanded public participation techniques; new options for public involvement through the Internet; EPA's emphasis on achieving compliance through partnerships, technical assistance, and public access to information; increased capacity of states, tribes and local governments to carry out delegated programs; and new government wide administrative procedures and public involvement requirements.[259]

---

[255] Id at 1-2.

[256] Id. at 2.

[257] Id. at 1, 3.

[258] Engaging the American People, A Review of EPA's Public Participation Policy and Regulations with Recommendations for Action. Prepared for the EPA Administrator by the EPA Public Participation Policy Review Workgroup, p v, (December 2000), http://www.epa.gov/publicinvolvement/pdf/eap_report.pdf (last accessed on August 3rd, 2014).

[259] Public Involvement Policy of the U.S. Environmental Protection Agency, p 3-4, May 2003 http://www.epa.gov/publicinvolvement/pdf/policy2003.pdf (last accessed on August 17, 2014).

The policy discussed above supplements what is already in place with respect to statutes like the Clean Water Act, the Resource Conservation and Recovery Act, and the Safe Drinking Water Act.[260] Generally, the EPA is required to make diligent efforts to involve the public in the environmental review process consistent with program regulations and EPA policies on public participation.[261] The responsible official shall ensure that public notice is provided for in accordance with 40 CFR 1506.6(b) and shall ensure that public involvement is carried out in accordance with EPA Public Participation Regulations, 40 CFR Part 25, and other applicable EPA public participation procedures.[262] 40 CFR 25(4) (b) (2) provides that each agency shall provide the public with continuing policy, program, and technical information and assistance beginning at the earliest practicable time. Such informational materials shall highlight significant issues that will be the subject of decision-making. Whenever possible, consistent with applicable statutory requirements, the social, economic, and environmental consequences of proposed decisions shall be clearly stated in such material.[263] Each agency shall identify segments of the public likely to be affected by agency decisions and should consider targeting informational materials toward them (in addition to the materials directed toward the general public).[264] Lengthy documents and complex technical materials that relate to significant decisions should be summarized for public and media uses.[265]

Fact sheets, news releases, newsletters, and other similar publications may be used to provide notice that materials are available and to facilitate public understanding of more complex documents, but shall not be a substitute for public access to the full documents.[266]

Each agency is required to develop and maintain a list of persons and organizations who have expressed an interest in or may, by the nature of their purposes, activities or members, be affected by or

---

[260] 40 CFR § 25.1.
[261] See. 40 CFR 6.400(a).
[262] Id.
[263] 40 CFR § 25.1.
[264] See id. at §25(4)(b)(2).
[265] Id.
[266] Id.

have an interest in any covered activity.[267] Generally, this list will be most useful "where subdivided by area of interest or geographic area.[268] This regulation also requires public notification, consultation, and public information concerning legal proceedings.[269] Public participation in the US extends beyond the pre-legislation, and goes to the post enforcement stage. That post enforcement stage involves the rights of victims of oil pollution to bring citizen suits against enforcement agencies like the EPA to enforce the laws in the statute books. One would hope that this American model is emulated by Nigeria.

The core elements of the EPA's New Public Involvement Policy are the following seven basic steps for effective public involvement:

1. Plan and budget for public involvement activities.
2. Identify the interested and affected public.
3. Consider providing technical or financial assistance to the public to facilitate involvement.
4. Provide information and outreach to the public.
5. Conduct public consultation and involvement activities.
6. Review and use input, and provide feedback to the public.
7. Evaluate public involvement activities.[270]

[267] See id. at §25(4)(b)(5).
[268] Id.
[269] Id. at § 25(4)(c),(d) & (e).
[270] 68 F.R. 33946-33949 http://www.gpo.gov/fdsys/pkg/FR-2003-06-06/html/03-14325.htm> (last accessed September 19, 2014), see also http://www.gpo.gov/fdsys/pkg/FR-2003-06-06/pdf/03-14325.pdf (last accessed September 19, 2014.

CHAPTER FOUR

1. Discussion of Regulatory Framework

1.A. Gas Flaring of Associated Natural Gas in Nigeria

When producing crude oil in Nigeria, extracted oil is usually mixed with natural gas. This natural gas is known as "associated natural gas." Most oil rich countries would like to export this natural gas because just like crude oil, it serves as a foreign exchange earner and because it is an alternative source of energy but many of them lack the technical know-how and technology so they resort to "Gas Flaring," which involves burning off the gas in order to concentrate on extracting the oil.

The most prudent way to treat natural gas is through re-injection. Re-injection involves returning the natural gas to the ground from where it came and this is important for two reasons. First, it ensures that the gas can be exploited in the future once the technology and technical know-how are in place thus preserving it for future generations. Second, it is environmentally friendly to re-inject.

In most villages in oil producing areas, dark or tranquil nights have become a thing of the past.[271] Most residents know that once the sun sets behind the mangroves, its light will be replaced by the glow from a roaring natural-gas flare close to the village's edge.[272] The fire pushes temperatures 10 to 30 degrees higher than the usual 90-plus readings in most swampy, tropical region of the oil producing areas.[273] The villagers' bizarre, round-the-clock coexistence with the giant torch may however be entering its final years.[274] Rising international demand for natural gas has sparked moves to capture

---

[271] See Greg Campbell, The Giant, Roaring, Gas Torch Next Door, The Christian Science Monitor, (Tuesday, May 1, 2001), http://www.highbeam.com/doc/1G1-73871856.html (last accessed on September 19, 2014).

[272] See id.

[273] Id.

[274] Id.

the fuel from Nigeria's flares rather than burn it as waste.[275] All six international oil companies operating in the Delta had initially committed to turning off their flares by 2008[276] but due to internal pressure from the oil communities and their supporters, the Nigerian government set the year 2004 as deadline for oil companies operating in the country to put an end to gas flaring.[277] The 2004 was unfortunately not met.

Some of the effects of the continuous flaring of gas in the oil producing areas include release of greenhouse gases into the atmosphere and acid rain.[278]The oil producing communities claim that the acid rain produced by the gas flaring has destroyed plant and wildlife.[279] Some of the diseases that have begun to manifest themselves among villagers exposed to gas flaring include respiratory diseases, cancer, cardiac diseases, tuberculosis, brain disorders, stroke, anemia, and high blood pressure.[280]

---

[275] Id.

[276] Id.

[277] See Emeka Duruigbo, Managing Oil Revenues for Socio-Economic Development in Nigeria: The Case for Community-Based Trust Funds, N.C. J. INT'L L. & COM. REG, Vol. 30, footnote 48, pages 123, 130, https://www.law.unc.edu/components/handlers/document.ashx?category=24&subcategory=52&cid=730 (citing, Abiodun Raufu, Nigerian Oil Workers & Families Rage Against Foreign Companies: Citizen Leaders Say Compensation Must Cover Health Damage from Four Decades of Gas Flaring, ECOTOPICS INTERNATIONAL NEWS SERVICE) <http://www.ecotopics.com/articles/nigerian_oil.htm> (last modified Sep. 20, 2004).

[278] See Joshua P. Eaton, The Nigerian Tragedy, Environmental Regulation of Transnational Corporation, and the Human Rights to a Human Environment, 15 B.U. Int'l LJ. 261, 269 (1997).

[279] Id. at 269.

[280] See Emeka Duruigbo, Managing Oil Revenues for Socio-Economic Development in Nigeria: The Case for Community-Based Trust Funds, N.C. J. INT'L L. & COM. REG, Vol. 30, footnote 48, pages 123, 130, https://www.law.unc.edu/components/handlers/document.ashx?category=24&subcategory=52&cid=730 (citing, Abiodun Raufu, Nigerian Oil Workers & Families Rage Against Foreign Companies: Citizen Leaders Say Compensation Must Cover Health Damage from Four Decades of Gas Flaring, ECOTOPICS INTERNATIONAL NEWS SERVICE) <http://www.ecotopics.com/articles/nigerian_oil.htm> (last modified Sep. 20, 2004).

1 .B. Regulatory Framework for Gas-Re-injection in Nigeria

A brief look at the Gas Reinjection regulations shows that the first regulation called the Associated Gas Re-Injection Act 1979 (No.99) stipulated that all flaring of associated natural gas should cease by January I, 1984, except with the permission of the minister.[281] This Act also made it obligatory for every company producing oil in Nigeria to submit detailed plans for gas utilization.[282]

In view of the limited domestic market for gas at the time and the high cost associated with gas development, the oil companies could not embark on any gas development program. Nigeria contains estimated proven oil resources of 22.5 billion barrels.[283] Since Government depends on oil production for her revenue, she had to review the 1979 Gas Re-injection Decree to enable the oil companies to produce oil, and thus consequently promulgated the Associated Gas Re-Injection (Continued Flaring of Gas Regulations 1984).[284] This regulation spelt out the conditions for the issuance of certificates by the Minister under Section 3(2) of the Associated Gas Re-Injection Act 1979 for the continued flaring of gas in a particular field or fields by companies engaged in the production of oil and gas.[285]

Next came the Associated Gas Re-Injection (Amendment) Decree No.7 of 1985 which was promulgated to deal with the problems arising from the implementation of the Associated Gas Re-Injection Act 1979.[286] A new subsection 2 in the amended Decree was substituted for subsection 2 of section 3 of the 1979 Act.[287] The 1985 Decree permits a company engaged in the production of oil and gas to continue to flare gas in a particular field or fields if the Minister

---

[281] See Section 3(1)-(2), Associated Gas Re-injection Act of 1979, Cap 26, LFN 1990.
[282] Id. at Section 2(1)-(2).
[283] NIGERIA: Oil Gas, Exploration laws and Regulations Handbook, at Page 71, Volume 1, Strategic Information and Regulations, International Business Publications ISBN 143307884-8.
[284] Id. at 71.
[285] Id. at 71.
[286] Id.
[287] Id.

issues a certificate to that effect and if he is satisfied after January 1, 1984 that utilization or reinjection of the produced gas is not appropriate or feasible in the particular field or fields.[288]

The certificate is subject to such terms and conditions as the Minister may impose.[289] The certificate may permit the company to continue to flare gas in a particular field or fields if the company pays such sum as the Minister may from time to time prescribe for every 28.317 standard cubic meter of gas flared.[290] The fee prescribed is eleven kobo per 28.317 standard cubic meter of gas flared.[291] Payments shall be made in the same manner and subject to the same procedure as for the payment of royalties by companies engaged in the production of oil i.e. in foreign currency.[292]

The low fines imposed on these companies does not create enough motivation for them to stop gas flaring. Oil firms in Nigeria, especially the international oil companies (IOCs), may continue to flare substantial amount of the gas resources in the country until 2020 which, according to them, is the feasible year for the flare out deadline.[293] Energy experts posit that the continued flaring of gas in the country amidst gas supply shortfall in the domestic market constitutes not only an environmental disaster, but also an economic tragedy.[294] The Federal Government has been trying to end natural gas flaring over the years but the flare out deadline has been repeatedly postponed with the most recent deadline being December 2012.[295] Before the latest deadline, as explained earlier there was a 2008 deadline. Eli Bala, Director-General and Chief Executive Officer, Energy Commission of Nigeria (ECN), speaking at the annual international conference of the Nigerian Association for

---

[288] Id.
[289] Id.
[290] Id.
[291] Id.
[292] Id.
[293] Femi Asu, Oil companies to continue to flare gas beyond 2015, Businessday (February 19, 2014), http://businessdayonline.com/2014/02/oil-companies-to-continue-to-flare-gas-beyond-2015/#.U_4O12N3ees (last accessed August 27, 2014).
[294] Id.
[295] Id.

Energy Economics (NAEE) on Tuesday, 11th, February, 2014, said that: "oil companies are still flaring a substantial amount of the natural gas in the country. According to the National Energy Policy (NEP), flaring was supposed to stop by 2008".[296] Bala, who was represented by Joseph Olayande, Director, Energy Planning and Analysis Department, ECN, said the NEP is currently being reviewed and they had considered that the next terminal date for gas flaring should be 2015. He added that consultation with oil companies and other stakeholders was ongoing, with the oil companies saying 2020 would be a more realistic deadline.[297]

One of the objectives of the policy statements in the NEP, which was approved in 2005, was to eliminate the flaring of associated gas by 2008 by encouraging the oil producing companies to gather and utilize the gas and by imposing appropriate and effective penalties to discourage gas flaring.[298] Emeka Duruigbo, Professor of Law at Thurgood Marshall School of Law, Texas Southern University, United States, said it was pathetic and horrible that gas was being flared in Nigeria. "The deadline keeps on shifting. Nigeria has tried to deal with this issue since at least since 1979, when they passed the Associated Gas, Re-injection Act and the regulations that follow and each time they imposed standards, fines, deadlines, nothing seems to come out of it".[299]

Nigeria is second to Russia in global gas flaring, according to the World Bank.[300] The country flared 536 billion standard cubic feet (scf) of natural gas in 2010, or about a third of the gross natural gas produced in 2010, according to the Nigerian National Petroleum Corporation (NNPC). In 2011, the NNPC claimed that flaring cost Nigeria $2.5 billion per year in lost revenue, according to the EIA.[301]

---

[296] Id.
[297] Id.
[298] Id.
[299] Id.
[300] Id.
[301] Id.

2.A. Federal Environmental Protection Agency Act (FEPA)

The Nigerian Federal Environmental Protection Agency Act (FEPA)[302] remains to date the most comprehensive environmental legislation passed in the country's history.[303] The dumping by an Italian firm of toxic waste in Nigeria in 1988 was the catalyst the government needed to enact the legislation after more than ten years of procrastination.[304] It established FEPA as the implementing authority with responsibility, among others, to establish environmental criteria, guidelines, and standards for the protection of the "nation's air and interstate waters as may be necessary to protect the health and welfare of the population from environmental degradation."[305]

FEPA was also mandated to make recommendations to the Minister with responsibility for the environment (currently the Minister of Environment) for the purpose of establishing water quality standards for the inter-state waters, to protect the public health or welfare and enhance the quality of water, taking into consideration the use and value for public water supplies, propagation of fish and wildlife, recreational purposes, agricultural, industrial and other legitimate uses.[306]

Section 20 of FEPA prohibited the "discharge in such harmful quantities of any hazardous substance into the air or upon the land and the waters of Nigeria" or adjoining shorelines except as permitted or authorized by any law in force in Nigeria. A violation of this prohibition secured a 100,000 naira fine ($606), ten years imprisonment, or both; where the offense is committed by a corporate body, the penalty was 500,000 naira ($3, 030) and an additional fine of 1,000 naira ($6.06) for every day the offense subsists.[307] In addition to criminal penalties, the owner or operator of

---

[302] Cap. 131, LFN 1990.
[303] Ambrose O.O. Ekpu, Environmental Impact of Oil on Water: A Comparative Overview of the Law and Policy in the United States and Nigeria, 24 Denv. J. Int'l L. & Pol'y 55, 84 (Fall 1995).
[304] Id. at 84.
[305] Id. (citing, §5(g) of FEPA).
[306] See. § 15 of FEPA.
[307] §5(g) of the FEPA.

the vessel or facility from which the discharge occurred was also liable for the costs of removal, restoration or replacement of natural resources destroyed as a result of the discharge, and "costs of third parties in the form of reparation, restoration, restitution, or compensation as may be determined by FEPA from time to time."[308] The owner or operator was, however, free from this additional liability if he or she could prove that the discharge was caused solely by a natural disaster, by an act of war, or by sabotage.[309] The discharger was also required to give immediate notice of the discharge to FEPA, begin "immediate cleanup operations," and promptly comply with other directions as FEPA may prescribe.

2. B. Shortcomings of FEPA

A legal commentator Ambrose Ekpu criticized the FEPA and suggested that it should be amended to cover not only hazardous substances but also oil because of the prevalence of oil spills in Nigerian waters.[310] In his view, the legislation that comes close to addressing the same concerns as FEPA in the US is the Comprehensive Environmental Compensation and Liability Act (CERCLA).[311]

Critics noted that the FEPA did not have the resources or the personnel to sufficiently monitor the Nigerian environment by itself.[312] It is imperative that the actual victims of ecological destruction be given the right to monitor their own environment and

---

[308] See. Ambrose O.O. Ekpu, Environmental Impact of Oil on Water: A Comparative Overview of the Law and Policy in the United States and Nigeria, 24 Denv. J. Int'l L. & Pol'y at 84.
[309] Id. at 84.
[310] Id. at 84.
[311] Id. at 84 (citing CERCLA, 42 U.S.C 9601).
[312] See Charles Marecic, How Many Wrongs Does It Take To Make A Human Right, 22 Vt. L. Rev. 20 L 215 (1997).

to have the power to sue violators for adequate compensation.[313] Even assuming that FEPA was made to apply to oil companies and although the legislation provided for some sanctions against the polluting companies and their managers, such sanctions neither provided a substantial deterrent effect against oil spills nor created any substantial incentives to clean up spills once they occur.[314] As previously discussed section 20(3) of the FEPA Decree imposed, in addition to the initial fine of up to approximately N500,000 ($3,030), for the discharge of harmful substances into the environment, only a N1,000 ($6.06) fine "for every day the offence subsists.[315] These amounts are a pittance to the foreign oil companies and their managers may opt to pay the daily fine and defer cleanup to some later undetermined time, instead of defraying cleanup costs at the time of the spill to the detriment of short-term profits. Section 20(4) of the FEPA Decree allowed the managers to avoid sanctions if they could prove either "that the offence was committed without their knowledge or that they exercised all due diligence to prevent the commission of such offence." The first defense provided a loophole for managers claiming ignorance of the offense, even if that ignorance was negligent, reckless, or even feigned.[316]

3. The National Environmental Standards and Regulations Enforcement Agency (NASREA) Act.[317]

On 17th May, 2007 and 30th May, 2007, the Nigerian Senate and the House of Representatives, respectively, passed the National Environmental Standards and Regulations Enforcement Agency (Establishment) Bill 2007.[318] On 30 July, 2007, the then Nigerian

---

[313] See. Ambrose 0.0. Ekpu, Environmental Impact of Oil on Water: A Comparative Overview of the Law and Policy in the United States and Nigeria, 24 Denv. J. Int' L. & Pol'y at 83.

[314] Id. at 83.

[315] See § 20(3) of the Federal Environmental Protection Agency Act. Cap 131 LFN. 1988 No 58.

[316] See id. at § 20(4).

[317] NASREA Act No. 25 of 2007, Cap N164 LFN 2007.

[318] Dr. S. Gozie Ogbodo, The National Environmental Standards and Regulations Enforcement Agency (NASREA) Act: A Review, at 1, Nigerian Law Guru,

President, Umaru Musa Yaradua, assented to the Bill, thus heralding the new law on environmental protection, hereinafter called the NESREA Act, 2007.[319] The NESREA Act repealed the Federal Environmental Protection Agency Act (FEPA Act) discussed previously thus becoming the primary law on environmental protection while the new agency replaced the old agency under FEPA.[320] The NASREA Act also tasked the agency with the enforcement of environmental standards, regulations, rules, laws, policies and guidelines.[321]

As a corporate entity the agency is endowed with perpetual succession and a common seal.[322] Pursuant to its responsibilities, it may sue and be sued in its corporate name.[323] Section 2 of the Act outlines the objectives of the agency and provides as follows:

> "The Agency, shall, subject to the provisions of this Act, have responsibility for the protection and development of the environment, biodiversity conservation and sustainable development of Nigerian's natural resources in general and environmental technology, including coordination and liaison with relevant stakeholders within and outside Nigeria on matters of enforcement of environmental standards, regulations, rules, laws, policies and guidelines. The Agency is armed with a wide range of powers with a view to making its operations more effective. In the sphere of environmental protection, the Agency can prohibit processes and use of equipment or technology that undermine environmental quality", it can also "conduct field follow-up compliance with set standards and take procedures prescribed by law against any violator."[324]

The Act empowers the agency to establish mobile courts to expeditiously dispense cases of environmental infringements.[325] However, this has to be done with the 'relevant judicial authorities'

---

http://www.nigerianlawguru.com/articles/environmental%20law/NATIONAL%20ENVIRONMENTAL%20STANDARDS%20AND%20REGULATIONS%20ENFORCEMENT%20AGENCY%20%28NESREA%29%20ACT,%20A%20REVIEW.pdf (last accessed August 31, 2014)

[319] Id. at 1.

[320] Id.

[321] Id at 1.

[322] Id.

[323] Id.

[324] Id. at 1-2.

[325] Id. at 2.

as well as in consonance with the Nigerian Constitution.[326] The Agency can conduct public investigations and make proposals to the Minister for the review of existing guidelines, regulations and standards on environment. It can develop environmental monitoring networks, and compile environmental data from other sectors, except the oil and gas sector.[327] In partnership with the public or private agencies, institutions and organizations, it can promote the expansion of research experiments, surveys and studies.[328]

With the approval of the Minister, the Agency can "establish programmes for setting standards and regulations for the prevention, reduction and elimination of pollution and other forms of environmental degradation in the nation's air, land, oceans, seas and other water bodies and for restoration and enhancement of the nation's environment and natural resources."[329] Through publications and other appropriate means, the Agency can collect and make available basic scientific data on environmental standards.[330] For their services, the Agency is empowered to charge fees.[331] Because the powers of the Agency does not extend to environmental issues arising from the oil and gas sector, the Agency lacks jurisdiction over environmental matters emanating from the oil and gas sector.[332] Also noteworthy is the fact that although the Agency has a Director-General as the Chief Executive Officer, it still remains, like its predecessor (FEPA), a parastatal within the Federal Ministry of Environment.[333] The Minister in charge of the Ministry enjoys an overriding authority over the Agency and its functions.[334]

In order to provide for effective enforcement of environmental standards, regulations, rules, laws, policies and guidelines by the newly established National Environmental Standards, Regulations

---

[326] Id.
[327] Id.
[328] Id.
[329] See id. at 2.
[330] Id.
[331] Id.
[332] Id. at 2.
[333] Id.
[334] Id.

and Enforcement Agency (NESREA),[335] the Minister of Environment is empowered to make regulations for the general purposes of carrying out or giving full effect to the functions of the Agency under the NESREA Act.[336]

By virtue of this power the following 24 Regulations, were made: National Environmental (Wetlands, River Banks and Lake Shores) Regulations, 2009; National Environmental (Watershed, Mountainous, Hilly and Catchment Areas) Regulations, 2009; National Environmental (Sanitation and Wastes Control) Regulations, 2009; National Environmental (Permitting and Licensing System) Regulations, 2009; National Environmental (Access to Genetic Resources and Benefit Sharing) Regulations, 2009; National Environmental (Mining and Processing of Coal, Ores and Industrial Minerals) Regulations, 2009; National Environmental (Ozone Layer Protection) Regulations, 2009; National Environmental (Food, Beverages and Tobacco Sector) Regulations, 2009; National Environmental (Textile, Wearing Apparel, Leather and Footwear Industry) Regulations, 2009; National Environmental (Noise Standards and
Control) Regulations, 2009; National Environmental (Chemical, Pharmaceutical, Soap and Detergent Manufacturing Industries) Regulations, 2009; National Environmental (Standards for Telecommunications and Broadcasting Facilities) Regulations, 2011; National Environmental (Soil Erosion and Flood Control) Regulations, 2011; National Environmental (Desertification Control and Drought Mitigation) Regulations, 2011; National Environmental (Base Metals, Iron and Steel Manufacturing/Recycling Industries Sector) Regulations, 2011; National Environmental (Control of Bush/Forest Fire and Open Burning) Regulations, 2011; National Environmental (Protection of Endangered Species in International Trade) Regulations, 2011; National Environmental (Domestic and

[335] Muhammed Tawfiq Ladan, 'National Environmental Regulations 2009 A New Dawn in Environmental Protection in Nigeria',8/1 Law, Environment and Development Journal (2012), p. 116, 127 http://www.lead-journal.org/content/12116.pdf (last accessed on September 6, 2014) (citing, Ladan M.T., (2009) Law, Cases and Policies on Energy, Mineral Resources, Climate Change, Environment, Water, Maritime and Human Rights in Nigeria. Ahmadu Bello University Press, Zaria, Nigeria, at pp. 357-378).

[336] See id. at 127 (citing section 34 of the NESREA Act No. 25 of 2007.)

Industrial Plastic, Rubber and Foam Sector) Regulations, 2011; National Environmental (Coastal and Marine Areas Protection) Regulations, 2011; National Environmental (Construction Sector) Regulations,2011; National Environmental (Control of Vehicular Emissions from Petrol and Diesel Engines) Regulations, 2011; National Environmental (Non-Metallic Minerals Manufacturing Industries Sector) Regulations, 2011; National Environmental (Surface and Groundwater Quality Control) Regulations, 2011; and National Environmental (Electrical/Electronic Sector) Regulations, 2011National Environmental (Wetlands, River Banks and Lake Shores) Regulations, 2009; National Environmental (Watershed, Mountainous, Hilly and Catchment Areas) Regulations, 2009; National Environmental (Sanitation and Wastes Control) Regulations 2009; National Environmental (Permitting and Licensing System) Regulations 2009; National Environmental (Access to Genetic Resources and Benefit Sharing) Regulations, 2009; National Environmental (Mining and Processing of Coal, Ores and Industrial Minerals) Regulations 2009; National Environmental (Ozone Layer Protection) Regulations, 2009; National Environmental (Food, Beverages and Tobacco Sector) Regulations, 2009; National Environmental (Textile, Wearing Apparel, Leather and Footwear Industry) Regulations, 2009; National Environmental (Noise Standards and Control) Regulations, 2009; National Environmental (Chemical, Pharmaceutical, Soap and Detergent Manufacturing Industries) Regulations, 2009.[337]

This statute is inapplicable to oil and gas pollution because of the express provision of the statute which excludes oil and gas pollution from the purview of the statute.

---

[337] See. Muhammed Tawfiq Ladan, 'National Environmental Regulations 2009 A New Dawn in Environmental Protection in Nigeria',8/1 Law, Environment and Development Journal (2012), at 127-128 http://www.lead-journal.org/content/12116.pdf (last accessed on September 6, 2014) (citing, Ladan M.T., (2009) Law, Cases and Policies on Energy, Mineral Resources, Climate Change, Environment, Water, Maritime and Human Rights in Nigeria. Ahmadu Bello University Press, Zaria, Nigeria, at pp. 357-378).

4.A. National Oil Spill Detection Response Agency Establishment Act (NOSDRA).

NOSDRA was passed into law in 2006. The law established NOSDRA as an Agency to be known as the National Oil Spill Detection and Response Agency with responsibility for preparedness, detection and response to all oil spillages in Nigeria as set out in section 5 of the Act.[338]The functions of NOSDRA include being responsible for surveillance and ensuring compliance with all existing environmental legislation and the detection of oil spills in the petroleum sector; receiving reports of oil spillages and coordinating oil spill response activities throughout Nigeria; coordinating the implementation of the Plan as may be formulated, from time to time, by the Federal Government; coordinating the implementation of the Plan for the removal of hazardous substances as may be issued by the Federal Government; performing such other functions as may be required to achieve the aims and objectives of the Agency under the Act or any plan as may be formulated by the Federal Government pursuant to this Act.[339]

4.B. The National Oil Spill Contingency Plan.

In order to give biting teeth to NOSDRA in 2009, a National Oil Spill Contingency Plan (NOSCP) which has existed on paper since the early 1980s was re-written and upgraded by stake-holders in the oil industry in order to make it effective. NOSDRA was given primary responsibility for its implementation and coordination.[340]

The Government of the Federal Republic of Nigeria stated that it recognizes the need to put in place an effective and tested crisis

---

[338] NOSDRA, Part II, section 2, Cap 157 LFN 2006.

[339] Id at Part III, section 6.

[340] See. The National Oil Spill Contingency Plan (NOSCP) for Nigeria, by The Sub-committee On Oil Spill Response of the National Action Coordinating Committee of the Forum for Cleaning-Up of The Niger Delta, at p 27, 4.0., Revised Edition May 2009, http://www.giwacaf.org/userfiles/contingency/18/Nigeria_NOSCP_2009_EN.pdf (last accessed September 6, 2014).

management capability through the National Oil Spill Contingency Plan.[341] The government said that this is in compliance with National Objective and the International Convention on Oil Pollution Preparedness, Response and Cooperation (OPRC 90) which Nigeria has ratified.[342] The OPRC 90 has been domesticated by the Merchant Shipping Act[343] as required by the Nigerian Constitution. The efforts to internalize some of its provisions on preparedness and response into the NOSCP indicates the readiness of the government to imbibe both the spirit and letter of the convention.

The overall goal of the National Policy on Environment is to achieve sustainable development through the following:

a) Securing for all Nigerians a quality of environment adequate for their health and well-being;

b) Conserving and using the natural resources for the benefit of the present and future generations;

c) Restoring, maintaining and enhancing the ecosystem and ecological processes essential for the preservation of biological diversity;

d) Raising public awareness and promoting understanding of the essential linkages between the environment and development, and;

e) Co-operating with other countries and international organizations to achieve (a) – (d) above and preventing trans-boundary environmental pollution.[344]

---

[341] Id. at p 27, 4.1.

[342] Id.

[343] Merchant Shipping Act, Cap M11 LFN 2004.

[344] The National Oil Spill Contingency Plan (NOSCP) for Nigeria, by The Sub-committee On Oil Spill Response of the National Action Coordinating Committee of the Forum for Cleaning-Up of The Niger Delta, at p 27, 4.2., Revised Edition May 2009, http://www.giwacaf.org/userfiles/contingency/18/Nigeria_NOSCP_2009_EN.pdf (last accessed September 6, 2014).

In view of the above, the National Policy advocates that exploration and production activities should be carried out in an environmentally sound manner with minimal disturbance to the natural environment where possible.[345] Accordingly, sustainable exploitation strategies to be implemented nationally in the oil and gas sector will, amongst other things, seek to:

a) ensure the implementation of the National Oil Spill Contingency Plan;

b) prepare a National Plan of Action for Awareness Preparedness for Emergencies at the local Level;

c) conduct spill modeling for all offshore developmental projects to enable proactive response to emergencies;

d) carry out inventory of spill sites and conduct prompt clean-up;

e) periodically inspect and ensure prompt maintenance of facilities as a proactive measure for prevention of oil spill;

f) encourage all mineral exploitation operators to keep accurate records of crude oil and product spills as well as other accidents that impact environmental quality and report them promptly to the appropriate authorities.[346]

The OPRC 90 directs, amongst others, that:-

Each party shall require that operations of offshore units under its jurisdiction have oil pollution emergency plans, which are coordinated with the national system established in accordance with article 6 and approved in accordance with procedures established by the competent national authority.[347] Each party shall require that authorities or operators in charge of such sea ports and oil handling facilities under its jurisdiction as it deems appropriate have oil pollution emergency plans or similar arrangements which are

[345] Id. at 27, 4.3.
[346] Id. at 28, 4.3.
[347] Id. at 28, 4.4.

coordinated with the national system established in accordance with article 6 and approved in accordance with procedures established by the competent national authority.[348]

In order to mitigate the adverse effect on the environment and the health of the people, of oil pollution arising from any spillages into the environment, the government recognizes three levels of oil spill contingency planning for the petroleum industry sector, namely:

(i) Company plans - Tier One

(ii) Cooperative plan – Tier Two

(iii) Government plan for major or disastrous oil spills – Tier Three.[349]

The NOSCP document claims that the company plans and cooperative plan are in place and functioning.[350] The NOSCP document notes that the first tier or company plan is mandatory for each producing and marketing company, the second tier, the cooperative or Clean Nigeria Associates (CNA) was formed by the producing companies to assist member companies in handling oil producing cases that an individual company is unable to combat.[351]

The government plan embodied in the national plan represents a third tier plan which provides for a response capability to major or disastrous oil pollution which is beyond the capabilities of individual oil companies first tier response, and the cooperative second tier response.[352]

The NOSCP put in place the above referenced tiered response system. It is imperative that the internationally accepted definitions

---

[348] Id. at 28.
[349] Id. at 21, 2.3.
[350] Id. at 21, 2.4.
[351] Id. at 21-22, 2.4.
[352] Id. at 22.

of oil spill categorization are clearly understood as they are essential in Tiered Response.[353]

Tier 1: Operational type spills less than or equal to 7 tons (50 bbls) that may occur at or near a company's own facilities as a consequence of its own activities.[354] An individual company is required under the OPRC 90 to provide resources to respond to this size of spill.[355]

Tier 2: A larger spill greater than 7 tons (50 bbls) but less than 700 tons (5000 bbls) may occur in the vicinity of a company's facilities.[356] Resources from another company, industry and possible government response agencies in the area can be called in on a mutual aid basis.[357] The company would participate in local co-operative such as the CNA where each member pools their Tier 1 resources and has access to any equipment which has been jointly purchased by the cooperative.[358]

Tier 3: The large spill greater than 700 tons (5000 bbls) where substantial further resources will be required and support from a national (Tier 3) or international co-operative stock pile, like the Oil Spill Response Limited (OSRL), may be necessary.[359] It is likely that such operation would be subject to government controls or even direction.[360] It is important to recognize that a spill which could receive a Tier 3 response may be close to, or remote from, company facilities.[361]

---

353 See. The National Oil Spill Contingency Plan (NOSCP) for Nigeria, by The Sub-committee On Oil Spill Response of the National Action Coordinating Committee of the Forum for Cleaning-Up of The Niger Delta, at p 64, 9.1., Revised Edition, May 2009, http://www.giwacaf.org/userfiles/contingency/18/Nigeria_NOSCP_2009_EN.pdf (last accessed September 6, 2014).

354 Id. at 64, 9.2.

355 Id.

356 Id. at 64, 9.3.

357 Id.

358 Id.

359 Id. at 64-65, 9.4.

360 Id. at 65, 9.4.

361 Id. at 65

The objectives of the National Oil Spill Contingency Plan (NOSCP) for Nigeria are as follows:

1. Establish a viable national operational organization that ensures a safe, timely effective and appropriate response to major or disastrous oil pollution, namely:

2. Establish a competent national authority, the National Oil Spill Detection and Response Agency (NOSDRA) with the responsibility for preparedness, detection and response to all oil spillages.

3. Identify high-risk areas as well as priority areas for protection and clean up.

4. Establish the mechanism to either monitor and assist or if necessary to direct the actual response, including the capability to swiftly mobilize the necessary resources to save lives, protect threatened environment, and clean up to the best practical extent of the polluted site.

5. Maximize the effective use of the available facilities and resources of individual companies, their international connections and oil spill cooperatives in implementing appropriate spill response.

6. Provide funding and appropriate and sufficient prepositioned pollution combating equipment and materials, as well as a functional communication network system required for an effective response to major oil pollution.

7. Provide a programme of activation, training and drill exercises to ensure readiness to oil pollution preparedness and response and also, the management and operational personnel.

8. Co-operate and/or provide advisory services, technical

support and equipment for purposes of responding to major oil pollution incident in West Africa sub-region upon request by the neighboring country, particularly where part of the Nigerian territory may itself be threatened.

9. Co-operate with relevant national and regional organizations, the International Maritime Organization (IMO) and other international organizations in the promotion and exchange of results of research and development programme relating to the enhancement of the state-of-the art of the oil pollution preparedness and response, including technologies, techniques for surveillance, containment, recovery, disposal, and cleanup to the best practical extent.

10. Establish agreements with neighboring countries regarding the rapid movement of equipment, personnel and supplies into and out of the countries for emergency spill response activities.

11. Determine and make vital combat equipment available at most strategic areas for rapid response.

12. Establish procedures by which Nigerian Customs and Immigration Services will enable rapid importation of extra, support response equipment and personnel.

13. Develop and implement an appropriate audit system for the entire organization.[362]

---

[362] See. The National Oil Spill Contingency Plan (NOSCP) for Nigeria, by The Sub-committee On Oil Spill Response of the National Action Coordinating Committee of the Forum for Cleaning-Up of The Niger Delta, at p 32-34, 6.1., Revised Edition May 2009, http://www.giwacaf.org/userfiles/contingency/18/Nigeria_NOSCP_2009_EN.pdf (last accessed September 6, 2014), see also NOSDRA, at Part III, section 5, Cap 157 LFN 2006.

The authority for the establishment of the National Oil Spill Contingency Plan derives from the following statutes:

a. Petroleum Decree No. 51, 1969. Section 8(1)(b) (iii)
b. The Petroleum (Drilling and Production) Regulations, 1969, section 25.
c. Government Administrative Directive (1981) for the Establishment of Three Levels of Oil Spill Contingency Plans (to effectively and promptly combat the various magnitude of pollution) namely; the Company plan, the Cooperative plan and the National Plan.
d. Federal Executive Council Approval and Formation at its 17th Council Meeting of 6 October, 1988, of a National Committee comprising relevant ministries, departments and organizations for the Formulation of the National Oil Spill Contingency Plan.
e. The Federal Environmental Protection Agency (FEPA) decree 58, 1988, section 22 & 23.
f. The National Policy on Environment which provides for the Establishment of a National Oil Spill Contingency Plan, and the
e National Oil Spill Detection & Response Agency (NOSDRA) Establishment Act No. 15 of 2006.[363]

In the National Oil Spill Contingency Plan, the following Government Ministries and Agencies have been identified as vital in the roles they will be expected to play in the event of a major oil spill disaster:

The Federal Ministry of Environment
The Ministry of Petroleum Resources
The Ministry of Defence (The Army, The Navy, The Air Force)
The Ministry of Foreign Affairs
The Federal Ministry of Works, Housing and Urban Development
The Federal Ministry of Transport
The Federal Ministry of Aviation
The Ministry of Communications
The Federal Ministry of Health
The Federal Ministry of Agriculture and Rural Development

363 Id. at 35-36, 6.3.1.

The Federal Ministry of Water Resources
The Federal Ministry of Information
The Federal Ministry of Science and Technology
The Nigerian National Petroleum Corporation (NNPC)
The Nigerian Institute of Oceanography and Marine Research
The Nigerian Police
The Nigerian Meteorological Agency
The National Emergency Management Agency (NEMA)
The Nigerian Ports Authority
The Nigerian Maritime Safety and Administration Agency (NIMASA)
The Oil Producers" Trade Section of the Lagos Chambers of Commerce (OPTS)
State and Local Governments
NGO"s and Communities
The Nigerian Red Cross Society
Industrial Groups and Academic Organizations.[364]

By the Executive Order that establishes Federal Ministry of Environment (FME), the FME is charged with the responsibility of ensuring a clean environment throughout Nigeria.[365] The FME is expected to protect Nigeria's environment against possible degradation by regulating the activities of industries in the country.[366] To this end, the National Oil Spill Detection and Response Agency (NOSDRA) as a Parastatal under the FME shall, in the event of a major or disastrous oil spill, in collaboration with other line agencies and responsible parties:-

a. Assess the extent of damage to the ecology by matching conditions following the spill against what existed before (reference baseline data and Environmental Sensitivity Index (ESI) maps).
b. Undertake a post-spill impact assessment to determine the extent and intensity of damage and long term effects.
c. Advise Government on possible effects on the health of the people and ensure that appropriate remedial action is taken

[364] Id. at 53-54, 7.1.
[365] Id. at 55, 8.1.
[366] Id.

for the restoration and compensation of the environment.

d. Assisting in mediating between affected communities and the spiller.
e. Monitor the response effort during an emergency, with a view to ensuring full compliance with existing legislation on such matters.
f. Assess any damage caused by the spill incident.
g. Urgently process and grant approval for any request made to it by the spiller for the use of approved dispersant or the application of any other technology considered vital in ameliorating the effect of the spill.
h. Advice and guide the response effort so as to ensure the protection of highly sensitive areas/habitats and the salvaging of endangered or threatened wild life.
i. Monitor the clean-up operations to ensure full rehabilitation of the affected areas.
j. The Chairman of the National Oil Spill Response Committee shall provide up-to-date information on the spill response efforts.[367]

The NOSCP stipulates that the National Oil Spill Detection and Response Agency (NOSDRA) shall act as the lead agency for all matters relating to oil spills response management and liaise with the Federal Ministry of Petroleum Resources for the implementation of NOSCP.[368] They are also members of the National Advisory Committee of NOSDRA.[369]

4.C. NOSCP ALERTING SYSTEM AND ACTIVATION

The National Plan will be considered activated upon the detection of any oil spill regardless of its size.[370] Following such detection, both the previously described report to government and an initial response

---

[367] Id. at 55-56, 8.1, see also NOSDRA Part IV section 19(1)(a)-(j).
[368] Id. at 56, 8.2.
[369] Id. at 56.
[370] Id. at 76, 13.1.

from the appropriate Tier level will be required.[371] Subsequently depending upon the spill situation, a higher Tier participation may be required.[372] The NOSCP emphasizes that the success of any and all response actions will depend on all parties understanding and operating within a chain of command structure with clearly defined relationships and responsibilities.[373]

4.D. NOSCP CHAIN OF COMMAND

The chain of command embodied in the National Oil Spill Contingency Plan represents a Tiered Response Plan which provides for a response capability to major or disastrous oil pollution which is beyond the capabilities of individual oil company's first response.[374] The chain of command thus integrates the three Tiers of contingency planning thus providing the necessary organizational structure, command and control, communication network and effective information service to ensure that government can be kept fully informed of all spill occurrences, monitor the spill response and intervene when required so as to cope with all spills which threaten the Nigerian environment.[375]

The NOSCP confirms that the National Oil Spill Detection and Response Agency (NOSDRA) is a parastatal under the Federal Ministry of Environment.[376] It states that NOSDRA shall be responsible for surveillance to ensure compliance with environmental legislation, as well as to detect oil spills, and monitoring, surveillance and co-coordinating spill response activities throughout the Federal Republic of Nigeria.[377] NOSDRA shall be headed by a Director General, appointed by the Ministry of Environment, and will based

---

[371] Id. at 76.
[372] Id. at 76.
[373] Id.
[374] Id. at 77, 14.1.
[375] Id.
[376] Id. at 77, 14.2.
[377] Id.

in the NOSDRA National Headquarters.[378] NOSDRA as a decentralized organization will delegate powers to the Zonal Centres in the Incident Command System (ICC).[379]

4.E. NOSCP -National Oil Spill Response Advisory Committee (NOSRAC)

The National Oil Spill Response Advisory Committee (NOSRAC) will be an advisory body within NOSDRA.[380] The members of this committee will be drawn from relevant ministries, departments, parastatals, and operators.[381] This Committee shall be a policy formulation body and as well shall act in an advisory capacity to the National Commander of NOSDRA in any situation in which the Organization is called upon for a response action.[382]

4.F. NOSCP - National Command and Control Response Centre (NCCRC)

The NOSCP states that the National Command and Control Response Centre (NCCRC), shall be established as a report processing and response coordinating center for all oil spill incidents, receiving all reports of oil spillages throughout the Federal Republic of Nigeria from the Zonal Command and Control Units of NOSDRA.[383] NCCRC shall serve as the command and control center for compliance monitoring of environmental legislation, surveillance for spill detection for monitoring and coordinating responses required in plan activations.[384] It shall be equipped with crisis management system including but not limited to the following

---

378 Id. at 77.
379 Id.
380 Id. 77, 14.3.
381 Id. at 77.
382 Id. at 78.
383 Id. at 78, 14.4.
384 Id. at 78.

accessories for:

a. Simulation Executive Network Control
b. Visual Systems
c. Performance Measurement Data Libraries
d. Geographic Information Systems (GIS)
e. Resources Data Base
f. Environmental Models
g. Incident Command System
h. Equipment Modeling
i. Cost Benefit Models
j. Data Base Management Systems
k. Early warning Spill Detection Buoys.[385]

The NOSCP states that for the purpose of reporting a spill, special predesignated telephone and communication systems such as e-mail, radio signals, fax, etc. shall be established as soon as this plan is in operation.[386]

---

[385] Id.
[386] Id. at 78.

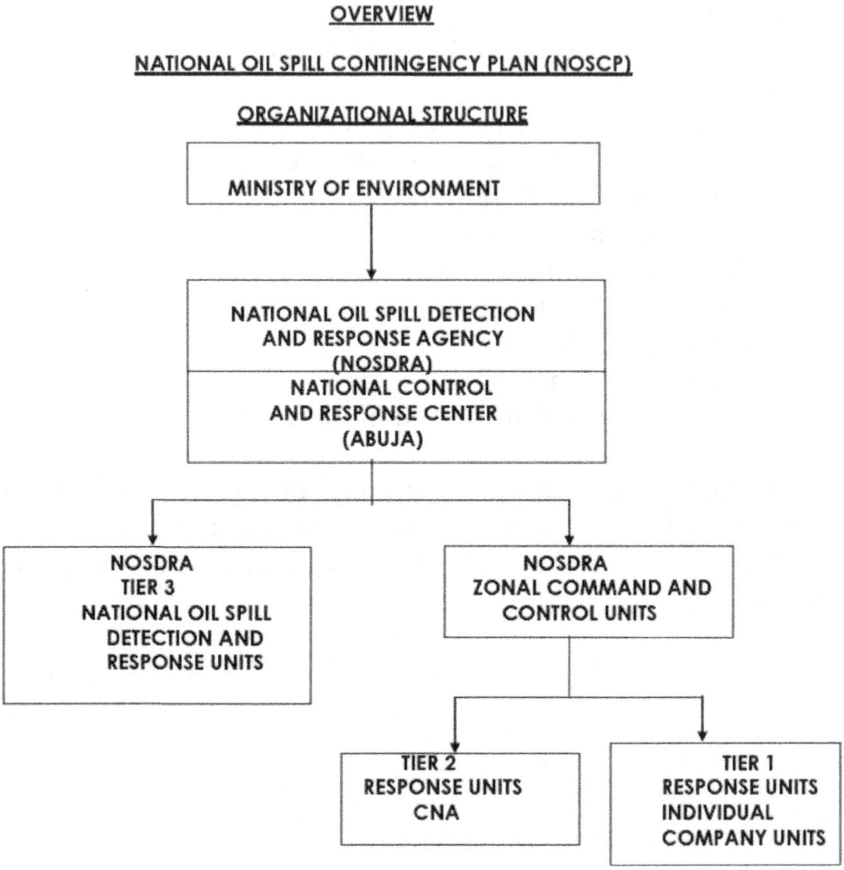

NATIONAL OIL SPILL CONTINGENCY PLAN (NOSCP) ORGANIZATIONAL STRUCTURE, FIGURE 10.1.[387]

[387] Id. at 67

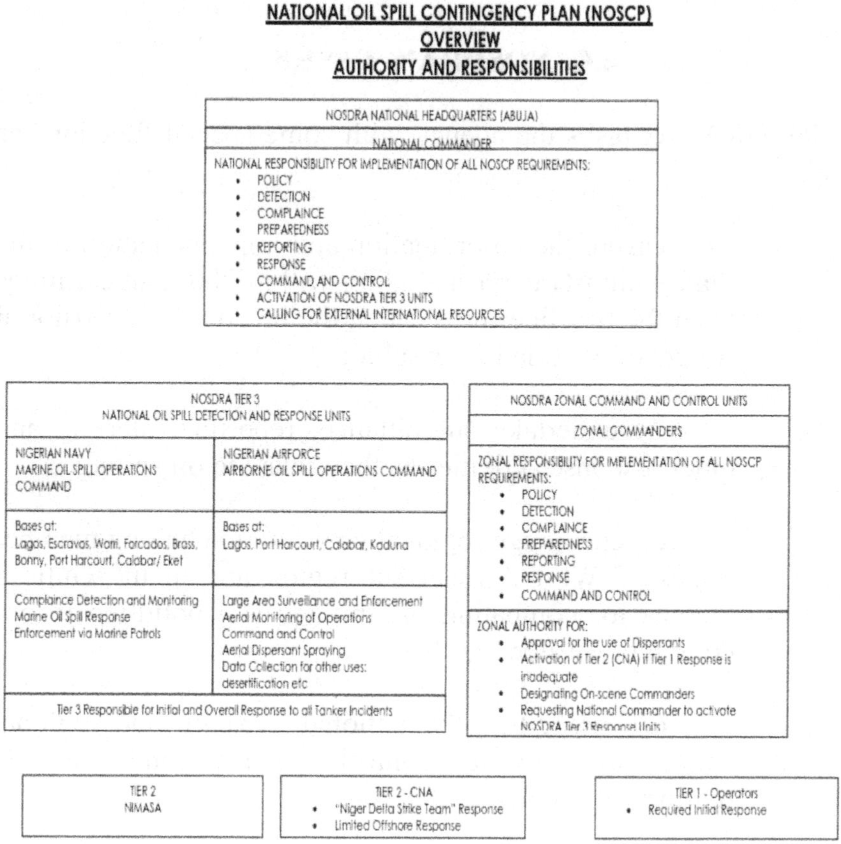

NATIONAL OIL SPILL CONTINGENCY PLAN (NOSCP) OVERVIEW AUTHORITY AND RESPONSIBILITIES, FIGURE 10.2.[388]

[388] Id. at 68.

4.G. NOSDRA'S TASKS

The NOSDRA Act tasks the agency with some special functions as follows:

"*(a)* ensure the co-ordination and implementation of the Plan within Nigeria including within 200 nautical miles from the baseline from which the breath of the territorial waters of Nigeria is measured;

(b) undertake surveillance, reporting, alerting and other response activities as they relate to oil spillages;

(c) encourage regional co-operation among member States of West African sub-region and in the Gulf of Guinea for combating oil spillage and pollution in our contiguous waters;

(d) strengthen the national capacity and regional action to prevent, control, combat and mitigate marine pollution;

(e) promote technical co-operation between Nigeria and member States of the West African sub-region;

(f) facilitate-

(i) the arrival and utilisation in and departure from Nigeria of ships, aircrafts and other modes of transport engaged in responding to oil pollution incidents or transporting personnel, cargo, materials and equipment required to deal with such an incident; and

(ii) the expeditious movement into, through and out of Nigeria of personnel, cargoes, materials and equipment;

(g) (i) the National Control and Response Centre shall for purposes of a Tier 3 oil spill response, undertake such functions as specified under section 20 of this Act;

(ii) the Director-General shall have the power to co-opt all the Government Ministries and Agencies mentioned under the Second Schedule to this Act, in the management of a Tier 3 or a major Tier 2 oil spill."[389]

4.H. NOSDRA's other functions

NOSDRA is mandated to cooperate with an oil spiller in the determination of appropriate measures to prevent excessive damage to the environment and the communities; expeditiously consider any proposal made for response effort by the oil spiller; mobilize internal resources and also assist to obtain any outside human and financial resources that may be required to combat any oil spill; and assist in the assessment of damage caused by an oil spillage.[390]

The second schedule to section 19(1)-(2) of the NOSDRA outlines specific duties for Ministries, Departments, and agencies such as the Ministry of Works, Ministry of Health, Ministry of Transport, Ministry of Information, Ministry of Communications, Ministry of Agriculture, Ministry of Aviation via NIMET, the National Emergency Management Agency, etc to perform in the event of an oil spill.

4.I. Criticisms of the NOSDRA Act 2006.

Senator Bukola Saraki, Chairman of the Senate Committee on the Environment and Ecology in his criticism of the NOSDRA Act explained that before the introduction of the motion for Amendment

[389] NOSDRA, at Part III, section 7, Cap 157 LFN 2006.
[390] Id at Part IV section 19(3)(a)-(d).

of the NOSDRA Act 2006 on September 19th, 2012, the Senate committee had consulted widely and at the time carried out on-the-spot-investigation, assessment and studies on the activities of multinational oil companies carrying out production activities in the Niger Delta region.[391]

Members of the committee include Benedict Ayade as Vice Chairman, Barnabas Gemade, and Ahmad Mohammed Sani Stores.[392] Others are Boluwaju Kunlere, Margery Okadigbo, Helen Esuene, Bukar Ibrahim, Gbenga Ashafa and the Chairman, Bukola Saraki.[393]

The committee was concerned that the NOSDRA 2006 Act has not helped in any meaningful way to arrest the impact of oil spills and gas flaring with its consequences on socio-economic life of oil producing communities.[394] This came against the backdrop of the gloomy narrative on the plight of the oil producing communities which includes the fact that oil spills in the oil producing communities of the Niger Delta region have done great harm to both the people and their ecosystem,[395] and the fact that the spillage is estimated at more than 15 million barrels, since oil production started in the late 50s in the region.[396] This is alarming because 15 million barrels is equivalent to about 55 times the volume of the Exxon Valdez oil spill in Alaska, United States in 1989 which was around 270,000 barrels and a little over three times the BP Gulf of Mexico oil spill of 2010 which was 4.76 million barrels in volume.

Senator Bukola Saraki, in an interactive session with officials of the National Oil Spill Detection Response Agency (NOSDRA), Civil Society Organizations (CSOs) and other stakeholders in the region

---

[391] By Dele Ogbodo, Niger Delta Oil Spills: Senate Takes the Gauntlet, Moves to Amend NOSDRA Act 2006, This Day Newspaper, This Day Live, (4 November 2012) http://www.thisdaylive.com/articles/n-delta-oil-spills-senate-takes-the-gauntlet-moves-to-amend-nosdra-act-2006/129571/ (last accessed September 7, 2014)

[392] Id.

[393] Id.

[394] Id.

[395] Id.

[396] Id.

stated that the situation on the ground today requires a more robust framework, which was why the Act in the past did not make the desired impact.[397] He said: "An effective legislative framework for oil spill management needs to go far enough to ensure that apart from remedying the environment, it can also provide enough deterrent for bad environmental behaviors.[398]

Senator Bukola Saraki stated further: "It should make spilling intolerable, for example the law, which stipulates a fine of not more than N1 million for oil spill, irrespective of the dimension and scope does not encourage environmental good behavior, neither does it create adequate disincentive to oil spilling and environment irresponsibility."[399]

The scathing criticisms of the NOSDRA and the subsisting NOSDRA Act by Senator Saraki appears justified when the activities of ExxonMobil in Akwa Ibom state and Shell in Ogoni land discussed in previous chapters is analyzed against the backdrop of the existence of the NOSDRA and the National Contingency Plan analyzed previously. Inadequate legislation does indeed encourage irresponsible environmental behavior, so also does refusal by those tasked with enforcement responsibility to enforce the legislation already on the books.

While trying to convince his colleagues on the need to expedite action on the amendment of the Bill, Saraki underscored the fact that oil spillage is not oil business but an environmental problem. He also stated that it does not necessarily have to be a consequence of oil exploration.[400] Oil spillage was described as an irresponsible environmental behavior on the part of the oil extracting companies.[401] The Senator said: "The fact that it is as a result of oil exploration does not detract from the impact on the environment."[402] He lamented that it is unfortunate that millions of Nigerians are struggling to make ends meet simply because their sources of

---

[397] Id.
[398] Id.
[399] Id.
[400] Id.
[401] Id.
[402] Id.

livelihood is impacted by what is going on in their land.[403] Painting a picture of the pathetic scenario, he stressed:

"The story is that of the destruction of the right of communities to live in a safe environment, to live decently and in good health. It will interest you distinguished Senators to know that Nigeria is one of the few very countries in the world not applying the polluter pay principle".[404]

"There is yet no legal framework for oil spill penalties.[405] The story is that of people with nowhere to run because nowhere is safe.[406] They turn to their waters for food the fishes are filled with carcinogenic hydrocarbons, turn to their farms the land can no longer produce even weed not to talk of food", he quipped.[407] According to him, the presence of oil spilt in these oil producing communities all these years have actually been ignored or neglected,[408] even though he acknowledged that oil spilt in a minority of cases may have been cleaned up.[409]

Senator Bukola Saraki referenced the United Nations Environmental Programme (UNEP) report which acknowledges that some of the spills of over 40 years in Nigeria's oil producing communities have not been cleaned up or remediated till date.[410] With the coming amendment, Saraki said companies found culpable in oil spill or gas flaring would be dealt with.[411]

Citing a recent example, he said: "In Brazil, Chevron and Transocean who already face a penalty of about R$20 billion an equivalent of US$11 billion for a spill of 3,500 barrels have seen prosecutors file criminal charges against the companies' employees."[412] These charges, Senator Saraki said could see the employees face up to 31 years in prison, adding that in August of 2012, a panel of judges in

---

403 Id.
404 Id.
405 Id.
406 Id.
407 Id.
408 Id.
409 Id.
410 Id.
411 Id.
412 Id.

Brazil upheld this penalty and temporarily revoked the licenses of these companies to operate in Brazil.[413]

In Nigeria, the Senator added that for a 400,000-barrels-spill, Nigerians plead extensively for clean-up and in several cases, government spends public funds to do the clean-up for the oil companies that are directly responsible for the oil spill.[414]

Citing the British Petroleum (BP) oil spill along the Gulf of Mexico as an example, Senator Saraki observed that BP contributed $15 billion to a joint fund with the United States government of about $20 billion before claims for compensation were made.[415] He noted that the BP have paid out $13 billion dollars to affected individuals to compensate for loss of profits.[416] In a Nigerian context based on what obtained at the time, Saraki mentioned that the affected individuals and families would have gotten bags of rice, beans blankets and bread.[417]

The crux of the new amendment to the Act lies in compelling oil companies to adequately pay for damages to the environment whether its gas flaring or oil spills, which result in environmental degradation.[418] He said Nigeria would lose in the region of over N44 billion due to an oil spill that occurred in Bonga known as the Bonga oil spills.[419] If the amendment is not passed, the Senator said the federal government would use taxpayers' money to clean up and remediate the environment.[420]

He said the bill would henceforth address the regulatory and legal framework, which is crucial to discouraging environmental bad behaviors that lead to oil spills and gas flaring in Nigeria.[421]

---

[413] Id.
[414] Id.
[415] Id.
[416] Id.
[417] Id.
[418] Id.
[419] Id.
[420] Id.
[421] Id.

Senator Bukola Saraki debunked the claim of the oil companies as to what they believe to be the true causes of oil spills in the oil producing communities of Nigeria. The oil companies told the committee that over 70 percent of the spillage is caused by indigenes through sabotage.[422] Saraki, however, said, "The statistics we have since authenticated suggest something different, that 50 percent of oil spills in Nigeria are due to corrosion of oil infrastructure including pipelines that are over 40-50 years old and therefore above integrity value.[423] 28 percent of the spills are determined to be as a result of sabotage, while 21 percent result from production operations."[424] He stated that negligence plays a major role in oil spills in Nigeria.[425] He pointed out that the committee's field enquiry and various comparative analyses indicate that unless we change the law on spill management in the country, the country will not make progress.[426]

Speaking further on the proposed amendments, Senator Bukola Saraki said the Senate is convinced that the amendment of the NOSDRA Act will significantly help rein in the unwholesome environmental practices which have made oil spills incessant in the Niger Delta.[427] He said: "Our aim is to make it more economical for operators to view and treat with respect the environment through deterrents.[428] The committee proposed under this bill, instruments that will help make it harder for polluters to dodge their responsibilities and compel them to pay compensation to individuals, families, communities who may be or are suffering from the impact of oil spills.[429]

The senator explained that they have in addition under this bill incorporated the establishment of a contingency fund which when established should help operate like the American superfund to provide cushion for managing the cost of oil spills especially ones with significant impact on the environment with the criteria that will

---

[422] Id.
[423] Id.
[424] Id.
[425] Id.
[426] Id.
[427] Id.
[428] Id.
[429] Id.

be developed as part of the Fund later."[430] He disclosed that under the amended NOSDRA Act, anybody whose interest is damaged by no fault of his should be able to get compensation.[431]

As of May 2013, the Committee had submitted its report for presentation and approval of the entire Senate and the Senate has taken the second reading of the bill to amend the NOSDRA Act, providing stiffer penalties for oil companies involved in both onshore and offshore spills.[432] If the bill becomes law, oil spillers will pay as high as N15bn as removal cost for spills occurring at any onshore facility, while those occurring offshore will attract a removal cost not less than N5bn.[433] The bill also stipulates the cost per barrel of oil spilled, depending on the vessels, facilities and places where the spills occur.[434]

A small tank vessel will attract not more than N50,000 penalty per barrel of oil spilled; the fine for a vessel that is less than 3,000 gross tonnes will be N100,000 per barrel; for a vessel above 3,000 gross tons, the penalty of N150,000 per barrel will apply; and any other vessel that does not fit into the description in the foregoing will attract a penalty of N250,000 per barrel.[435]

The penalties are contained in four new proposed sections (8, 9, 10 and 11) inserted as amendments in the principal Act.[436]

In addition, Section 8(9) of the proposed amended NOSDRA Act states,

"Notwithstanding the limitations established in section 8(1), all removal costs incurred by the Federal Government of Nigeria or any

---

[430] Id.
[431] Id.
[432] NOSDRA Amendment Act: Oil Spill to attract N15b Fine, Nigerian Energy Intelligence (September 20th, 2012) http://nigeriaenergyintelliegence.blogspot.com/2012/09/nosdra-amendment-act-oil-spill-to.html (last updated September 7th 2014)
[433] Id.
[434] Id.
[435] Id.
[436] Id.

state, local government, person or agency in connection with a spill or substantial threat of a discharge of oil or gas from any facility or vessel carrying oil or gas cargo from such a facility shall be borne by the owner or operator of such facility or vessel."[437]

Section 8(7) of the proposed amendment bill states that the failure to clean up the impacted site by a spiller, to all practical extent including the submission of action plan for remediation within two weeks of the occurrence of the spill shall constitute an offence and upon conviction the oil spiller shall be liable to a fine not less than N3,000,000 per day the spill is not cleaned up or to imprisonment for a term not exceeding 3 years or an amount up to 3 times the costs incurred by the agency as a result of such failure.

Section 11(a)(i) of the proposed amendment bill states that "A responsible party to a spill shall be liable in compensation for damages to real or personal property, loss of subsistence use of natural resources, loss of profits and earning capacity due to injury, destruction, of personal property or natural resources, severance and opportunities both private and public in nature arising as a result of an oil spill or unauthorized gas release or the removal cost.

Section 11(i) of the proposed amendment bill expands the categories of people who can bring claims of damages and compensation against a responsible party for an oil spill by providing that individuals, communities, states, government body, corporations and any other entity claiming genuinely for damage or loss as a result of an oil spill within Nigeria and Nigeria exclusive economic zone or such other jurisdictions within the control of the government of Nigeria may make a claim for compensation jointly or severally.

5. The Oil in Navigable Waters Act.

The attempt to regulate oil pollution from vessels or ships in Nigeria is worth comparing with that of the U.S. The comparison is relevant despite the huge technological and economic disparities between the

[437] Id.

two nations. Since oil transportation is a global industry, industry players should be expected to adopt the same standards and technology worldwide for the uniform protection of all waters from oil pollution. Oil transportation via tanker-vessels is a global industry that applies a uniform standard for determining freight rates regardless of where it is being transported. Thus, it can be asserted that the tanker-vessel owners or chatterers make the same profits from their operations no matter where the oil is coming from.

However, Nigeria's experience in replicating operations of other countries reveals that in the absence of a strict and viable regulatory regime, tanker-vessel owners will use unseaworthy vessels which have outdated safety and navigational equipment to transport crude-oil and other petroleum products to and from Nigeria. Another consequence of not having a robust and regulatory regime like that of the US is that the Protection & Indemnity Clubs (P & I Clubs) which are primarily responsible for insuring ship or vessel owners against oil spill liabilities might be able to deny insurance coverage to a bankrupt ship-owner who is unable to pay for liabilities in the event of an oil spill based on specific clauses in the insurance contract.

The major law governing oil pollution in US waters is the Oil Pollution Act of 1990[438] and unlike its Nigerian equivalent, this law imposes strict liability on the owner and operator of a vessel or facility that discharges oil into US waters. It only provides for three defenses to liability namely act of war, act of God, and the act of a third party not in any contractual relationship with the owner of the ship.[439]

The Nigerian law on the contrary which is briefly discussed below provides a long list of defenses. Unlike Nigeria, the US statute provides for numerous categories of private causes of action for damages for oil pollution.[440]

[438] 33 U.S.C. §2701-2761.

[439] 33 U.S.C. §2703.

[440] 33 U.S.C. §2702(b)(2):"Damages The damages referred to in subsection (a) of this section are the following: (A) Natural resources Damages for injury to, destruction of, loss of, or loss of use of, natural resources, including the reasonable costs of assessing the damage, which shall be recoverable by a United States

Unlike the Nigerian law, US law requires the polluter to clean up the oil spill.[441] The Nigerian legislature should take a cue from the US approach and reform its archaic law. If the proposed amendments to NOSDRA discussed earlier is passed by the Nigerian National Assembly then some of the criticisms of the Oil in Navigable Waters Act of 1968 (OINWA) would have been addressed by the law.

The oil in Navigable waters Act of 1968 (OINWA)[442] has remained the only legislation devoted to oil pollution of Nigeria's waters. Its scope is unfortunately severely limited and it appears to have outlived its relevance. It was enacted not so much out of the government's concern for the environmental well-being of Nigerians, nor to protect navigable waters from oil pollution, but rather to fulfill the government's desire to comply with its international obligation under the International Convention for the Prevention of Pollution of the sea by Oil.[443]

OINWA provides in section 1 that it shall be an offence for any Nigerian ship to discharge oil (which was defined to include crude oil, fuel oil, lubricating oil, and heavy diesel oil) or any mixture

---

trustee, a State trustee, an Indian tribe trustee, or a foreign trustee. (B) Real or personal property Damages for injury to, or economic losses resulting from destruction of, real or personal property, which shall be recoverable by a claimant who owns or leases that property. (C) Subsistence use Damages for loss of subsistence use of natural resources, which shall be recoverable by any claimant who so uses natural resources which have been injured, destroyed, or lost, without regard to the ownership or management of the resources. (D) Revenues Damages equal to the net loss of taxes, royalties, rents, fees, or net profit shares due to the injury, destruction, or loss of real property, personal property, or natural resources, which shall be recoverable by the Government of the United States, a State, or a political subdivision thereof. (E) Profits and earning capacity Damages equal to the loss of profits or impairment of earning capacity due to the injury, destruction, or loss of real property, personal property, or natural resources, which shall be recoverable by any claimant. (F) Public services Damages for net costs of providing increased or additional public services during or after removal activities, including protection from fire, safety, or health hazards, caused by a discharge of oil, which shall be recoverable by a State, or a political subdivision of a State." 33 U.S.C. §2702(b)(2).

[441] 33 U.S.C. §2702.

[442] Cap. 337, LFN 1990.

[443] The Convention was subsequently amended in 1962, 1969 and 1971. The preamble to the Act clearly confirms the motive for passing it.

containing not less than 100 parts oil into a part of the sea which has been declared a "prohibited sea area," attracting a fine for the owner and master of the ship not exceeding 2,000 naira (Nigerian currency that is currently about 165 to 1 US dollar) on summary trial. Furthermore, the OINWA makes it an offence for any person to discharge oil, or mixture containing oil, into waters from "any vessel, or from any place on land, or from an apparatus used for transferring oil from or to any vessel.[444] Section 3(2) of the Act provides that this applies to the whole of the sea within the seaward limits of the territorial waters of Nigeria; and all other waters (including inland waters) which are within those limits and are navigable by sea-going ships. The offence relates to discharge of oil into all the navigable waters of Nigeria which include all navigable inland waters and the whole of the sea within the seaward limits of the country's territorial waters which at present stands at 30 nautical miles from the coast of Nigeria.[445] It appears that the foregoing provisions are meant to exclusively regulate discharge of oil in the course of navigation and the discharges from such operations as bunkering and other cases of transfers of oil from vessels to places on land and vice versa.

To ensure compliance, the Act further empowers the Minister of Transport to enact regulations requiring masters of Nigerian ships of 80 tons gross tonnage or more to keep records in a prescribed form, in respect of every discharge of oil under any circumstance.[446] Sundry offences are created in relation to the keeping of records ranging from failure to report discharges to the keeping of false or misleading records.[447] The penalties vary from fines not exceeding 1,000 naira to imprisonment not exceeding six months or both.[448] To further encourage compliance, the Act empowers every harbor authority in the country to provide oil reception facilities to enable vessels to discharge or deposit oil residues.

The above provisions appear very impressive on the surface but a closer examination of its provisions reveals that the sting was taken

---

[444] Cap. 337 LFN 1990, § 3(1), see also CAP 06 LFN 2004.
[445] The Territorial Waters (Amendment) Act No. 38 of 1971.
[446] Cap. 337 §§ 7, 9 & 10.
[447] §7(5)(a)-(b).
[448] §7(5)(b).

out of the enactment in two important respects. Firstly, Section 4 states that it shall be a defense to any charge of unlawful discharge of oil if the oil was discharged for the purpose of securing the safety of any vessel, or of preventing damage to any vessel or cargo or of saving life.[449] The act can also be defended if it can be shown that the discharge was due to an escape in the consequence of a damage to the vessel.[450] Where oil has been discharged into waters from a place on land, it shall be a defense to prove that the oil escaped without want of reasonable care on the part of the occupier or that it was due to the act of a third party trespasser provided that as soon as practicable after the escape was discovered all reasonable steps were taken for stopping or reducing it.[451]

Surely by the time all these defenses are invoked, it is hardly possible to convict anybody under the provisions of the enactment. The statute also regrettably endorses the negligence standard of liability instead of the strict liability standard.

Another severe restriction on the effectiveness of the OINWA as an oil pollution statute is the stipulation contained in Section 12 that no action can be brought under the Act except with the consent of the Attorney General of the Federation. This no doubt is going to cause delays in the prosecution of cases under the enactment and may even diminish the enthusiasm of enforcement officials to enforce the law.

---

[449] §4(1).
[450] §4(2)(a).
[451] Id. at §4.

CHAPTER FIVE

1. Comparing the regulatory framework in Nigeria to that of the U.S. and its effect on the Responsible Party and its P & I Club

A. OINWA provides for grossly inadequate sanctions:

The amount stipulated as fines in the OINWA is grossly inadequate. While under the United States Oil Pollution Act (OPA) a tanker-vessel of over 3,000 gross tons, may be required to pay $10m for the costs associated with a spill,[452] in Nigeria it only needs to pay 2,000 naira (which is currently about 12 US dollars). This invariably drastically reduces the burden on the P & I Clubs and tanker owners who do business in Nigerian waters.

B. OINWA's plethora of outdated statutory defenses and policy defenses that polluters and their P & I Club can rely on:

The defenses that the OINWA allows a responsible party or his P & I Club to invoke are outdated and ought to be discarded. It attaches more importance to the cargo and vessel rather than the environment because it allows the discharge of fuel for the purpose of securing the safety of the vessel, or of preventing damage to the vessel or cargo.

It also allows the defense that the spill was caused by the acts of a third party trespasser unlike the OPA which stipulates that 'the acts of a third party who is an agent and employee of the responsible party shall not exculpate him.'[453] The OINWA exculpates a responsible party for acts of third parties who fall into these categories. This makes it easy for a tanker-vessel owner or his P & I Club to avoid liability under the Act. Unlike the OPA which limits the defenses of the responsible party or his P & I Club to those provided under the Act, the Oil in navigable waters Act does not do so. The implication of this is that a P & I Clubs can easily avoid liability if they can successfully raise any of their policy defenses.

---

[452] 33 U.S.C §2704.

[453] 33 U.S.C. §2703 (a).

Therefore, the burden of paying for cleanups will rest on the government and indirectly the taxpayers.

C. OINWA limits the right of action:

The Act severely hampers the right of a private victim of an oil pollution incident to bring legal action against a responsible party. The Act's provision which only allows a right of action against a polluting vessel where the Minister gives his consent severely hampers the right of the victims of oil spills to a fair hearing. This is the exact opposite of the OPA which allows new claimants (who had prior to OPA been denied a right of recovery in common law) to proceed against a responsible party.[454]

D. OINWA does not provide for the right of direct action against P & I Clubs:

The OINWA does not provide for direct action against oil spill insurers or guarantors unlike the OPA.[455] Consequently, if a ship owner becomes insolvent, no claimant can proceed directly against the ship owner's insurers or guarantors despite the fact that they have collected premiums from the ship owner. The victims of such oil spill will then have to depend on the benevolence of the P & I Clubs, since they have the discretion to decide whether or not to pay under those circumstances in their rules.

E. OINWA has no 'polluter pays' principle:

---

[454] Id. at § 2702(b).

[455] See 33 U.S.C § 2716(f)(1): "(f) Claims against guarantor (1) In general Subject to paragraph (2), a claim for which liability may be established under section 2702 of this title may be asserted directly against any guarantor providing evidence of financial responsibility for a responsible party liable under that section for removal costs and damages to which the claim pertains. In defending against such a claim, the guarantor may invoke-- (A) all rights and defenses which would be available to the responsible party under this Act; (B) any defense authorized under subsection (e) of this section; and (C) the defense that the incident was caused by the willful misconduct of the responsible party. The guarantor may not invoke any other defense that might be available in proceedings brought by the responsible party against the guarantor." 33 USCA § 2716.

Unlike the OPA,[456] the OINWA does not impose a strict duty on oil polluters to pay for oil spill clean-up costs. There is an undue emphasis on punishment or minute criminal fines (12 US dollars at the current exchange rate) instead of focusing on the cataclysmic effect that oil spills have on the environment. Considering the fact that most of the multinational oil companies operating in Nigeria are highly capitalized, the amount of the fines is not only embarrassing to the country but highly inappropriate. These fines will only engender irresponsible behavior of ship owning companies, ship operating companies, and oil companies.

F. OINWA does not establish an oil spill clean-up fund and a response program:

Unlike the OPA,[457] OINWA does not establish an oil spill clean-up fund thus placing the burden of clean-up of oil spills exclusively on overburdened tax-payers. There is no requirement that oil companies pay a certain percentage of their oil revenue to a fund dedicated to paying for damages and the clean-up of oil spills. No response program is provided for under the statute. Therefore when an oil spill occurs, government agencies responsible for environmental protection will not be ready for it. The vessel itself will also be ill prepared to respond to an oil spill emergency. The adoption of the NOSCP in 2009 discussed earlier in chapter four could in theory change this if its provisions are implemented. However, previous discussions on the ineffectiveness of both the NOSDRA Act and

---

[456] See. 33 USCA § 2702 (a): "(a) In general Notwithstanding any other provision or rule of law, and subject to the provisions of this Act, each responsible party for a vessel or a facility from which oil is discharged, or which poses the substantial threat of a discharge of oil, into or upon the navigable waters or adjoining shorelines or the exclusive economic zone is liable for the removal costs and damages specified in subsection (b) of this section that result from such incident."

[457] See. 33 U.S.C. 2712: This section makes a Fund of $1 billion available for the payment of private and public claimants when there is an oil spill. The fund is derived from a five cents per barrel levy on oil that is imported into the United States. Nigeria could take a cue from this and this could be a way to reduce the incessant tension between the major oil companies and the oil producing communities. Subsection (f) of this section provides that payment of any claim or obligation by the Fund under this Act shall be subject to the United States Government acquiring by subrogation all rights of the claimant or State to recover from the responsible party.

NOSDRA when it comes to oil spill response in relation to the NOSCP makes implementation of the NOSCP a dim prospect unless there is legislative intervention and an overhaul of the implementation capabilities of NOSDRA.

G. OINWA does not allow private or public causes of action for damages:

Unlike the OPA which allows for government trustees, private claimants, and governments claimants to sue for damages, OINWA does not expressly allow any cause of action for damages. It does not permit anyone to sue a polluter for damages occasioned by the loss of natural resources nor does it allow law suits for damages for injury to or economic losses resulting from destruction of real or personal property. It does not allow damages for loss of subsistence use of natural resources; damages equivalent to the net loss of taxes, royalties, rents, fees or net profit shares due to the injury, destruction or loss of real property, personal property or natural resources. It does not allow recovery for damages resulting from the loss of profits or impairment of earning capacity due to the injury, destruction or loss of real or personal property or natural resources; and damages for the net cost of providing increased or additional public services during or after removal activities.

The illuminating discussion of the weak and outdated regulatory framework in Nigeria reveals that there is a compelling need for a new legislation to protect the waters of Nigeria against oil pollution and to compensate the victims of marine pollution. It is also important for such legislation to borrow some of the good provisions of the OPA. If the amendments to NOSDRA discussed previously are passed into law and rigidly enforced, then some of these concerns may become a thing of the past.

CHAPTER SIX

1. International Treaties in relation to oil pollution in Nigeria

International Convention on Civil Liability for Oil Pollution Damage (CLC)[458] has been ratified by the Nigerian government. It was enacted due to the international community's consciousness of the dangers of pollution posed by the worldwide maritime carriage of oil in bulk,[459] and of the need to ensure that adequate compensation is available to persons who suffer damage caused by pollution resulting from the escape or discharge of oil from ships.[460] This Convention applies exclusively to pollution damage caused on the territory including the territorial sea of a signatory state and to preventive measures taken to prevent or minimize such damage.[461]

The Convention defines "oil" as any persistent oil such as crude oil, fuel oil heavy diesel oil, lubricating oil and whale oil, whether carried on board a ship as cargo or in the bunkers of such a ship.[462] "Pollution damage" is defined as loss or damage caused outside the ship carrying oil by contamination resulting from the escape or discharge of oil from the ship wherever such escape or discharge may occur, and includes the costs of preventive measures and further loss or damage caused by preventive measures.[463]

This convention limits the liability of a ship owner to a certain amount. Because the limitation amount was inadequate, another international treaty called Convention on the Establishment of an International Fund for Compensation for Oil Pollution Damage (IOPC) was passed in 1971. This was an additional funding provided through contributions made by all persons who receive oil by sea in signatory states.

---

[458] International Convention on Civil Liability for Oil Pollution Damage (Brussels, 29 November 1969).
[459] Id.
[460] Id.
[461] Id. at Art II.
[462] Id. at Art I (5).
[463] Id. at Art I (6).

Nigeria ratified the 1969 CLC and 1971 IOPC Fund Conventions. Section 12(1) of the 1999 Constitution of Nigeria, provides that treaties only become law after it is domesticated by an Act of the National Assembly. Such a treaty only becomes law if it is ratified by a majority of the National Assembly in the Federation.[464] The National Assembly of the Federal Republic of Nigeria is made up of the Senate and the House of Representatives. These two conventions were domesticated by the National Assembly via the Merchant Shipping Act,[465] and is therefore law in Nigeria.

The ratification and the domestication of these protocols could in theory go a long way in ensuring that removal costs of oil spills and damages are recoverable by those injured by oil spills in Nigeria. It could in theory also make the establishment of a separate domestic oil spill fund unnecessary.

If the executive branch of government finds that the Federal legislature is determined to tackle the pandemic of oil pollution in Nigerian waters head on, then it could sponsor a bill to repeal the OINWA, by borrowing heavily from OPA's provisions with slight modifications as articulated earlier. However, adopting a clone of OPA without slight modifications is still much better than the current law because an OPA clone would create a domestic Oil Spill Fund bigger than the International Fund and drastically reduce the defenses available to a polluter.

---

[464] See 1999 Constitution of the Federal Republic of Nigeria, Part 2, §12(3).

[465] Merchant Shipping Act, Cap M11 LFN 2004, Section 336(1)(i).

CHAPTER SEVEN

1. Best Available Technology as a Preventive Measure against Oil Spills.

The only subsisting Nigerian legislation that deals with the use of technology that enhances cleaner environment is the NASREA Act. Section 24(1) of the NASREA Act[466] provides that "the NASREA shall establish effluent limitations for new point sources which shall require application of the best control technology currently available and implementation of the best management practices." Under section 24(2), "the Agency is also required to establish effluent limitations for existing point sources which shall require the application of the best management practices under circumstances as determined by the Agency. This section also requires the agency to include schedules of compliance for installation and operation of the best practicable control technology as determined by the Agency."

Section 24(3) of the NASREA Act exempts the oil and gas sector from the regulatory reach of the NASREA when it comes to adopting the best control technology currently available but empowers the Agency to make superseding regulations on effluent limitations, on existing and
new point sources, for the protection of human, animal, marine and plant life.

It is unfortunate that these same provisions on use of the best available technology was not written into the NOSDRA legislation which empowers NOSDRA to regulate the activities of the oil and gas industry exempted from NASREA's regulatory reach. A counter argument may be made that other oil and gas government agencies such as the Department of Petroleum Resources would work to ensure that the best available technology is used based on existing legislation that it relies on in its regulatory activities.

This counter argument is weak because these agencies have a history of looking the other way when oil companies commit infractions of the existing regulations and this explains why the oil producing

---

[466] NASREA Act No. 25 of 2007, Cap N164 LFN 2007.

communities of the Niger Delta have become a negative example of how not to allow multinational oil companies operate in a country. These agencies have a reputation of siding with the multinational oil companies in opposing stricter anti-oil pollution legislation and regulations. It is unlikely that they will support strict regulations of the multinational oil companies in the near future.

As a result of the weak enforcement of existing oil and gas pollution regulations and the non-adoption of very strict regulations that empower NOSDRA to police the standard and quality of the equipment the oil companies use, the multinational oil companies still use old and environmentally unfriendly technology. They still use technological equipment that would not be allowed in the United States and other developed countries. Their pipelines are also very old and outdated and would not meet United States standards, especially with regard to their thickness and maintenance requirements as well as the depth to which the pipelines should be buried in the ground. The same thing applies to the loading technology that they use at the terminals at which crude oil is loaded to vessels for transportation to buyers of Nigeria's crude oil.

2. Environmental Impact Assessment in Nigeria

Environmental impact assessment is the formal process used to predict the environmental consequences (positive or negative) of a plan, policy, program, or project prior to the decision to move forward with the proposed action.[467] The International Association for Impact Assessment (IAIA) defines an environmental impact assessment as "the process of identifying, predicting, evaluating and mitigating the biophysical, social, and other relevant effects of development proposals prior to major decisions being taken and

[467] Environmental Impact Assessment, Wikipedia https://en.wikipedia.org/wiki/Environmental_impact_assessment (last accessed on October 14, 2014)

commitments made."[468]

A hypothetical example will help in the understanding of this issue. For instance, Exxon Mobil wants to lay pipelines across farmlands and streams or canals in some villages in oil producing areas to transport crude oil from an oil flow station to the refinery. It is assumed that most of the inhabitants of these oil producing areas are farmers and fishermen who also depend on farm products and the marine life for subsistence living. In order for the government to allow the pipelines to be laid, Environmental Impact Assessment (EIS) is required to examine the potential impact of the project on every facet of the environment, i.e. the project's impact on the water and its habitat, on the farm land, human health, and the air.

The Environmental Impact Assessment Act 1992 (EIA Act)[469] is the only Nigerian law governing the issue of Environmental Impact Assessment (EIA). The EIA Act specifically says:

"(1) The public or private sector of the economy shall not undertake or embark on or authorize projects or activities without prior consideration at an early stages of their environmental effects.

(2) Where the extent, nature or location of a proposed project or activity is such that is likely to significantly affect the environment, its environmental impact assessment shall be undertaken in accordance with the provisions of this Decree

(3) The criterion and procedure under this Decree shall be used to determine whether an activity is likely to significantly affect the environment and is therefore subject to an environmental impact assessment.

(4) All agencies, institutions (whether public or private) except exempted pursuant to this Decree, shall before embarking on the

---

[468] Id (citing Principle of Environmental Impact Assessment Best Practice, International Association for Impact Assessment, p 2 (1999) http://www.iaia.org/publicdocuments/special-publications/Principles%20of%20IA_web.pdf (last accessed October 14, 2014)
[469] See EIA Act Cap E12, LFN 2004

proposed project apply in writing to the Agency, so that subject activities can be quickly and surely identified and environmental assessment applied as the activities are being planned."[470]

The Environmental Assessments Department of the Federal Ministry of the Environment is the Agency responsible for approval and monitoring of the EIA process. Unfortunately, despite the statutory requirements of the EIA Act, EIA is nothing other than a myth in Nigeria where oil companies embark on extensive projects without conducting it. Even though they do conduct occasionally, most critics see it as mere public relations. It is also interesting to note that many countries have been much more successful in regulating the environmental practices of the same transnational oil companies that wreak havoc in Nigeria.[471]

To compare Shell's conduct in Europe with its conduct in Nigeria, Greenpeace International related the events surrounding Shell's construction of a pipeline in Scotland.[472] For that project alone, seventeen environmental surveys were commissioned and Shell produced a "painstakingly detailed Environmental Impact Assessment covering every meter of the route.[473] Many of Shell's operations and materials in Nigeria "would be illegal in other parts of the world.[474] This legal treatise already discussed in chapter one, the brazen manner in which ExxonMobil disregarded the warnings in its own EIA about the damage the implementation of the Yoho project would do to the pristine marine environment of the people of Eastern Obolo and other surrounding areas. The EIA predicted that the Yoho project if embarked upon by ExxonMobil was likely to cause the flora and fauna of those communities to be retarded. Despite this grim assessment, ExxonMobil still embarked on the project which has devastated and still devastates the pristine marine environment of the communities referenced in the EIA.

---

[470] See § 2 EIA Act.
[471] See Joshua P. Eaton, The Nigerian Tragedy, Environmental Regulation of Transnational Corporation, and the Human Rights to a Human Environment. 15 B.U. Int'l L.J. 261, 283 (1997).
[472] Id. at 283.
[473] Id.
[474] Id.

Another good example is the 620 miles (1,033 kilometers) West Africa Gas Pipeline (WAGP) from Nigeria to a gas-fired power plant in Ghana which was in its planning stages some years ago.[475] Some of the gas was also to be utilized by Benin and Togo, countries the pipeline was to pass through.[476] In February 2003, the four nations signed an agreement on the implementation of the WAGP. The treaty, which is for a 20-year period, provides for a comprehensive legal, fiscal and regulatory framework, as well as a single authority for the implementation of the project.[477] The WAGP partners are Chevron-Texaco with 36.7%, NNPC with 25%, Shell with 18%, Ghana's Volta River Authority (VRA) with 16.3% and SoBeGaz and SoToGaz each with a 2% interest.[478]

In June 2002, a Bank-funded gas-fired power plant in Ghana, Takoradi power plant, signed a gas supply agreement.[479]The gas was expected to significantly reduce boiler-fuel costs at Takoradi by substituting gas for oil.[480] In 2009 the first natural gas supply through WAGP arrived in Ghana.[481] In the same year Ghana's Volta River Authority generated electricity with natural gas from WAGP.[482]

The road leading to the completion of the project was very rough. Community representatives rejected the project and opposed public funding by the World Bank.[483] They demanded an inclusive environmental impact assessment of the WAGP, citing concerns about pollution, deforestation, pipeline explosions, and habitat

---

[475] United States Energy Information Administration, West African Gas Pipeline (WAGP) Project, http://www.eia.gov/emeu/cabs/wagp.html (last updated March 2003 and now archived).
[476] Id.
[477] Id.
[478] Id.
[479] Id.
[480] Id.
[481] Website of the West African Gas Pipeline Company, http://www.wagpco.com/index.php?option=com_content&view=article&id=46&Itemid=78&lang=en (last accessed on July 12, 2014).
[482] Id.
[483] United States Energy Information Administration, West African Gas Pipeline (WAGP) Project, http://www.eia.gov/emeu/cabs/wagp.html (last updated March 2003 and now archived).

fragmentation.[484] The communities alleged that the pipeline could also displace as many as 50,000 people along the route.[485]

Some commentators pointed out that while the introduction of mandatory EIAs is an encouraging development, the inability of local people to validate many of the assessments limits their effectiveness.[486] They further noted that a recent Greenpeace report asserts that while "oil companies' operations in developed regions are usually accompanied by environmental impact assessments, social and environmental policies, and a great deal of effort to appease the justified concerns of local communities, these practices are not exported to lesser developed regions, where little or no media attention is paid and where accountability is unheard of."[487]

In response to the concerns of these communities, the World Bank undertook an EIS in 2004, and consulted with people that they referred to as "community leaders."[488] The reason an EIS was conducted was probably because the World Bank was involved in the funding of the project and because the World Bank's modern practice is to conduct an EIS for environmentally sensitive projects of that size. They identified these community leaders as mostly Obas[489] or traditional rulers and acknowledged in their assessments that the project would disrupt the economic well-being of communities in Lagos State and Ogun State,[490] and that it will require the destruction of grave sites and cultural sites in the affected

---

[484] Id.

[485] Id.

[486] Emeka Duruigbo, Owen Wozniak, and Michelle Leighton, Oil Development in Nigeria: A critical investigation of Chevron Corporation's performance in the Niger River Delta, CALIFORNIA GLOBAL CORPORATE ACCOUNTABILITY PROJECT, The Nautilus Institute for Security and Sustainable Development, p 10 (2001).

[487] Id.

[488] See. NIGERIA FINAL DRAFT REV 1, Resettlement Action Plan –Nigeria West African Gas Pipeline, p 43, 74, 91, 142, Prepared for West African Pipeline Company (June 2004), <www-wds.worldbank.org/servlet/WDSContentServer/WDSP/IB/2004/08/26/000112742_20040826141211/Rendered/PDF/rp2540v30Nigeria0RAP0June02004.pdf> (last accessed on June 29th 2014).

[489] Id at 91.

[490] Id. at 179.

communities.[491] They also acknowledged that many people would lose their homes and farmlands to the project.[492] In their resettlement assessment, they claimed that they consulted with these community leaders, but one wonders if their consultation was with only the Obas and Chiefs. One wonders if they consulted directly with the individuals whose houses were in danger of being taken away by eminent domain and all its attendant complications.

They also stated that the pipelines pass under about 32 roads and three major highways across Lagos State and Ogun State, and also is made to pass under the sea floor, right by some of the pristine Lagos beaches.[493] This of course raises a lot of safety and environmental concerns like the danger that the pipelines pose to motorists and pedestrians that pass over these pipelines in cases of pipeline explosions. Most of the roads in Lagos State at the time were in a serious state of disrepair, and having pipelines running under these types of roads, pose a serious danger to motorists. Most Nigerians have seen what pipeline fire can do to people. If there is a rupture of the pipelines in the ocean floor near the beaches due to corrosion, sabotage or terrorism, that could pose an ecological disaster of cataclysmic proportions, because the strong waves of the sea could spread the leaking gas across the sea and thereby destroy the pristine environment of the beaches before the operators are able to shut off the gas flow or block the leakage. Of course, natural gas is not as destructive as oil, but it will still have an impact on the marine environment.

The U.S. has an Environmental Impact Statement Program in place. The National Environmental Policy Act (NEPA)[494] demands the filing of an environmental impact statement (EIS) by all Federal agencies on "proposals for legislation and other major Federal actions significantly affecting the quality of the human environment.[495] Federal actions include actions of private parties with Federal authorization or permits. The permit could include one

---

[491] Id. at 182.
[492] Id. at 179.
493 Id. at 55, 60, 63.
[494] See 42 USC §§4321 - 4370.
[495] Id. at § 102(2)(C).

for the laying of pipelines.

There are two main distinctions between the position in the US and Nigeria. First, the US utilizes an Environmental Impact Statement which is driven by alternatives (this means that the government agency could suggest a different method or location) compared to Nigeria which utilizes Environmental Assessment. This means that the communities affected by the Gas pipeline project got a take it or leave it proposal, and had no choice but to accept whatever was proposed. Second, the US enforces its Environmental Impact Statement requirements, while Nigeria does not enforce its EIA Decree.

3. Corporate Self-Regulation in the Oil Industry

The United States Exxon Valdez disaster which spilled 10.8 million gallons of crude oil onto the ecologically sensitive Alaskan coast in 1989, provided a sacrificial lamb for the environmental movement and launched a flurry of corporate and non-profit environmental activity.[496] Rapidly responding to the disaster, the Coalition for Environmentally Responsible Economies (CERES) announced the Valdez Principles, ten guidelines for environmentally responsible behavior.[497] In 1990, CERES began to bombard Exxon and other Fortune 500 corporations with shareholder resolutions urging them to sign the Valdez Principles.[498] Although corporate America responded negatively toward signing the Valdez Principles, there was a positive response toward the concept of environmentally responsible behavior.[499] By the end of the year, the "greening" of the industry was well underway.[500]

In response to the call for international standards and industry

---

[496] Pamela S. Evers, ISO 14000 AND ENVIRONMENTAL PROTECTION 67 Miss. L.J. 463 (Winter 1997).
[497] Id. at 463.
[498] Id.
[499] Id.
[500] Id. at 463-464.

involvement, the International Organization for Standardization (ISO) coordinated the efforts of 118 nations in delineating a set of protocols for the implementation of a comprehensive environmental management system known as the ISO 14000 series.[501] On September 3, 1996, the ISO completed and published the ISO 14001 and 14004 environmental management standards, the first of an evolving series of protocols referred to collectively as ISO 14000.[502] ISO 14000 places concern for the environment squarely onto the desks of business executives and government officials as a voluntary call to action.[503] In other words the ISO 14000 is bold move beyond environmental compliance into the world of corporate self-regulation.

The ISO 14 000 has developed more than 350 international standards (out of a total of more than twelve thousand) for the monitoring of such aspects as the quality of air, water, and soil.[504] These standards are a means of providing businesses and governments with scientifically valid data on the environmental effects of economic activity.[505] They also serve in a number of countries as the technical basis for environmental regulation.[506]

The oil companies in Nigeria should internalize ISO 14000 requirements in their principles of operation mainly because of the problem of the weak enforcement of environmental regulations which are in themselves inadequate.

4. CONCLUSION

One thing that is evident from the analysis of the legal framework in both the US and Nigeria is the fact that the approach of the former is markedly distinct in quality or character from that of the latter. This

---

[501] Id. at 466.
[502] Id.
[503] Id. at 466-467.
[504] See. ISO 14000 Meet The Whole Family, at 3, http://elsmar.com/pdf_files/iso14000.pdf (last accessed June 5th, 2014).
[505] Id. at 3.
[506] Id.

marked distinction in quality must be put in its proper context. The over-reliance of Nigeria on oil revenue may not permit it to put in place the most effective normative framework and the best enforcement mechanism.

The most important thing for Nigeria to do is to start enforcing the laws that it has even though they are grossly inadequate. What Nigeria needs is a twin edged approach of enforcing the subsisting legal regime and simultaneous reformation of same.

Made in the USA
Monee, IL
04 November 2026

67377033R00056